Harald Jes

Lizards

With photography by
well-known animal
photographers
Illustrations:
Johann Brandstetter

BARRON'S

CONTENTS

Typical Lizards 4

Factors to Consider 6

Acquiring a Lizard and Getting It Settled 9

Natural History 9

Lizards in the Terrarium 9

TIP: Terrarium Size 11

TIP: Species Conservation 15

Table: Which Lizards Can Live Together? 19

Where to Get a Lizard 21

Selecting the Right Lizard 21

Checklist: Buying a Lizard 21

HOW-TO: Getting Your Lizard Settled 22

Proper Care and Feeding 25

The Terrarium 25

Ventilation 25

Terrarium Technology 26

Heating 26

Lighting 26

Temperature and Humidity 27

Plants in the Terrarium 28

Plant Care 28

Desert Plants 28

HOW-TO: Housing 30

Rainforest Plants 32

Ten Golden Rules for a Healthy Lizard 33

Basic Terrarium Maintenance 34

Climate Control 34

Cleaning the Terrarium 34

Grooming 35

Vacation Care 35

A Healthy Diet 36

Plants in the Diet 36

Insects in the Diet 36

Vitamins and Minerals 37

HOW-TO: Feeding 38

Lizard Breeding 40

TIP: Sex Determination 43

Observing and Understanding Lizards	45	Preventive Care and Health Problems	53	Index	60
Body Temperature	45	Your Lizard's Health	53	Information	62
The Limbs	45	Handling Lizards Correctly	53	ASK THE EXPERTS	64
The Skin	45	Treating Illnesses	54		
TIP: Observing Lizards	46	TIP: Fecal Examinations	55		
The Sense Organs	46	Table: Recognizing Health Problems	58		
Typical Features and Behavior Patterns	46				
Behavior Guide	48				
TIP: Housing Lizards Together	50				
Avoiding Stressful Situations in the Terrarium	51				

TYPICAL LIZARDS

- Are found in temperate zones worldwide, from the desert to the tropical rainforest.
- Adapt to varied habitats in fascinating ways.
- Live in trees or on the ground.
- Regularly shed their skin.
- Lay eggs or give birth to live offspring.
- May be active by day or by night.

Lizards live all around the world, in climate zones ranging from temperate to tropical. Individual species have developed many fascinating adaptations to their various habitats. For example, most geckos have microscopic hooked cells on the undersides of their toes, enabling them to scamper not only along smooth leaves, but even up glass surfaces and across ceilings. A chameleon can move its eyes independently in all directions—astonishingly, it can even see forwards and backwards at the same time. An interesting defensive maneuver of many lizards is to shed the tail, which continues to twitch for a time, thus diverting the predator's attention from the lizard itself. All lizards, however, have one thing in common: In contrast to our warm-blooded house pets, such as cats and dogs, lizards are cold-blooded creatures whose body temperature varies with the temperature of their surroundings.

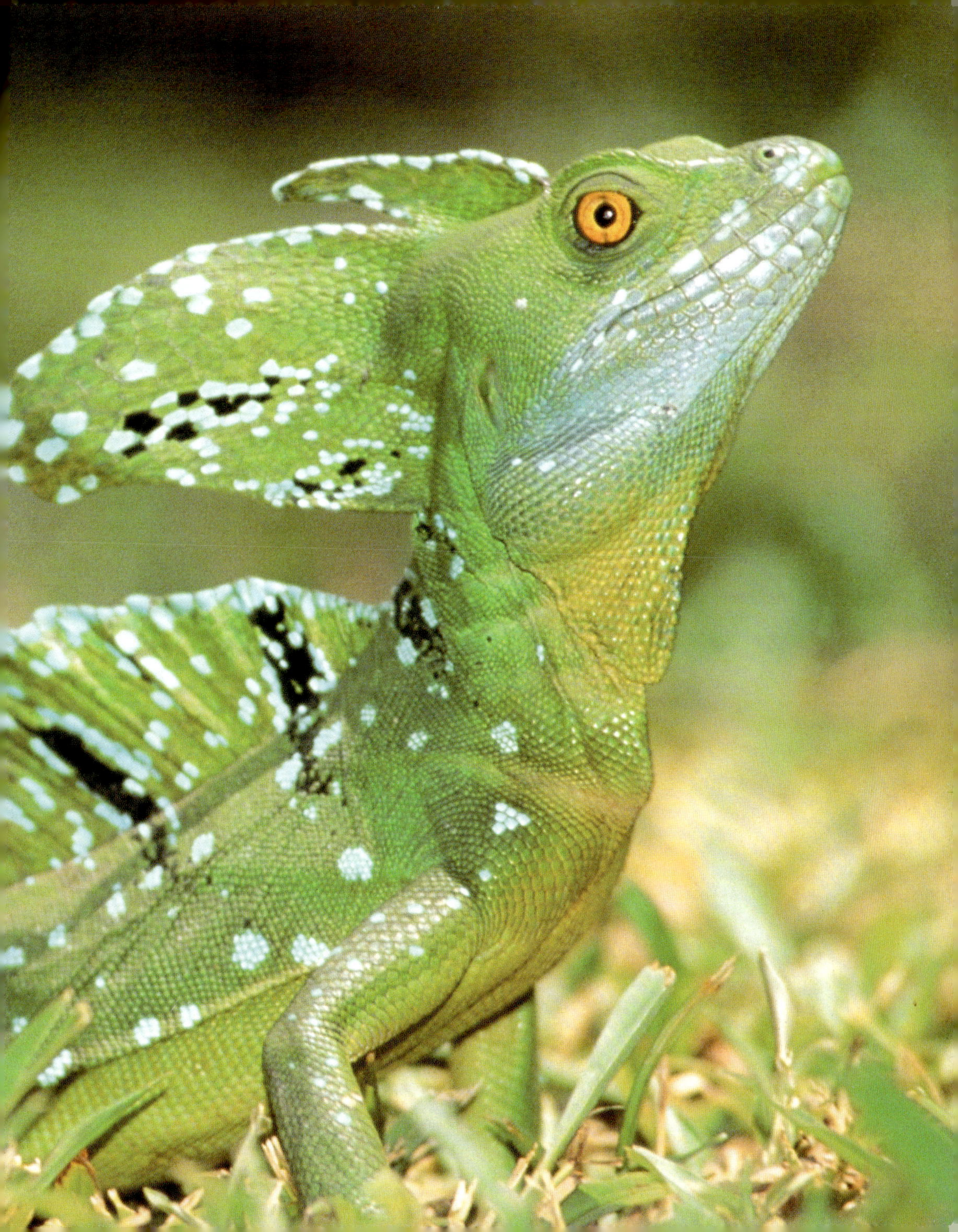

FACTORS TO CONSIDER

1 Lizards are generally not good companion pets. They don't like to be handled or stroked. In rare cases, lizards of the larger species may become tame.

2 Lizards are not suitable pets for small children. Don't bring a lizard home until your child understands that lizards are not toys or playmates.

3 Almost all the lizards that are available for purchase belong to tropical or subtropical species. Therefore, the conditions in the terrarium must be carefully controlled. The right equipment makes this possible, but it's expensive.

4 Another expense you must plan for is veterinary care if your pet lizard should get sick. Be sure you have identified a specialist in your area who is knowledgeable about lizards and their care.

5 Not every person is comfortable with feeding animals to a pet. Before you choose a lizard, think about whether you'd rather have a vegetarian or a meat-eater.

6 Pet lizards need attention even when their owners are on vacation. You will need a reliable person to tend the terrarium while you're away.

Think Carefully Before You Buy

Many lizards can live more than 20 years. Therefore, you should be well aware that keeping a lizard involves a long-term responsibility. Although daily care takes relatively little time, you should plan to spend a good amount of time observing your lizards, so that you can learn as much as possible about their behavior. Also, it's important to be sure that other family members are willing to accept a lizard in the household. There's the possibility that the creature will escape from the terrarium; some lizards tend to be noisy at night; and if the terrarium is not cleaned on a regular basis, it will smell.

Fortunately, there are no indications that lizards cause allergies in humans. Nevertheless, of course, proper hygiene should be observed.

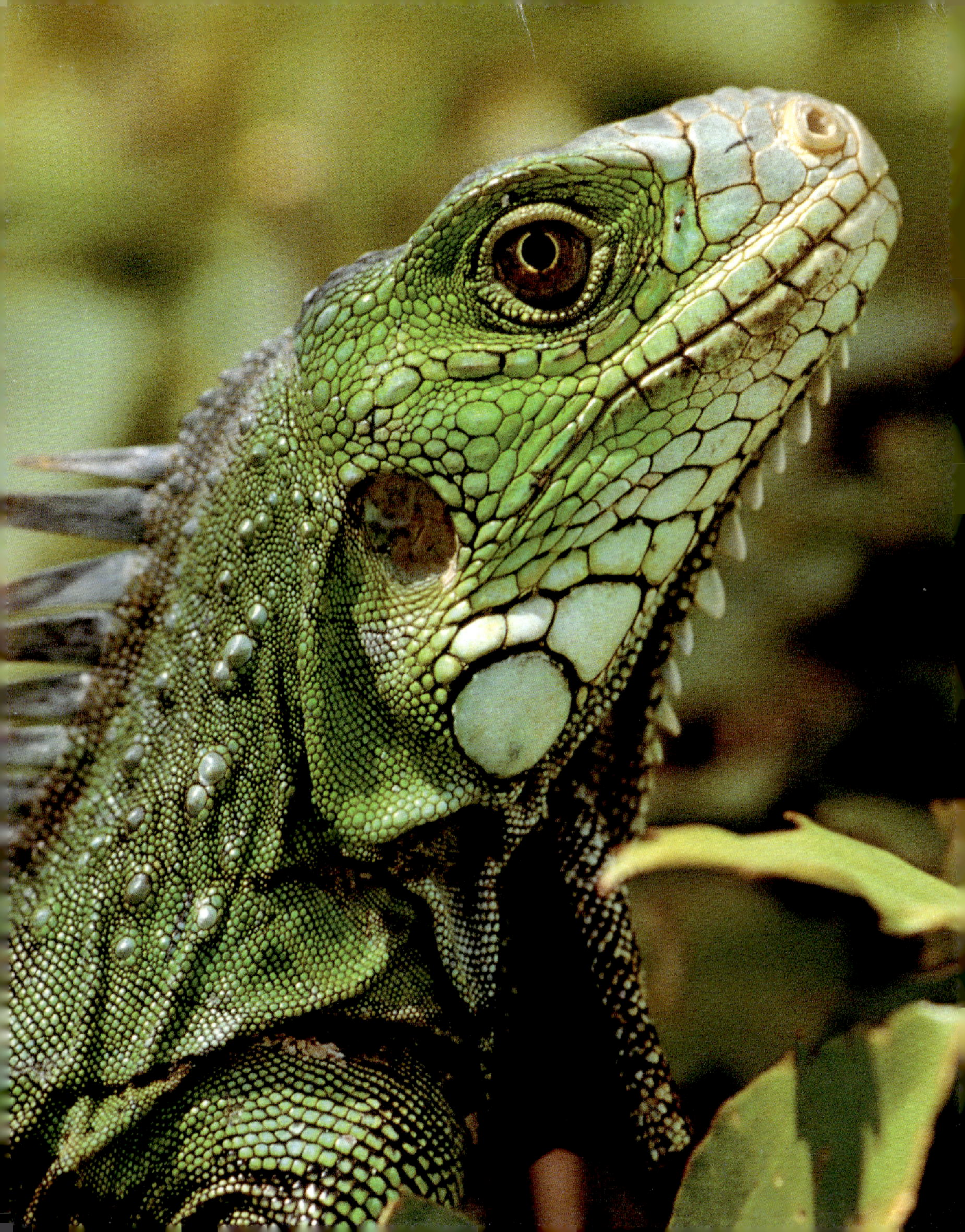

ACQUIRING A LIZARD AND GETTING IT SETTLED

With their scaly skin, their mostly immovable eyes, and a circulatory system that does not provide the body with warmth, lizards call to mind the saurian reptiles of times long past. Keeping these primeval creatures in a terrarium can be a fascinating hobby, but it also demands specific knowledge.

Lizards, which belong to the class Reptilia, are often less familiar to us than mammals or birds. However, anyone who wants to keep lizards in a terrarium should know what they are like and where they come from. Lizards' body structure, behavior, and living habits provide the lizard-keeper with important indications for their care and maintenance.

Natural History

Fossil finds provide evidence that the first lizards were on the earth 260 million years ago—in the Upper Carboniferous period. But because by this time they already existed in many forms, it is clear that there had been a common ancestor earlier.

The precursors of present-day lizards first appeared 100 million years ago, during the Cretaceous period.

Where Lizards Live Today

Lizards are found throughout the temperate zones of the earth, though most species live in

The green iguana is active by day and lives on trees in tropical rain forests and savanna trees.

the tropical zones. The species that live in areas of human occupation may be threatened in their natural habitat, and many are under special protection. (See TIP: *Species Conservation*, page 15.)

Lizards in the Terrarium

The lizards included here are species that are easily bred in captivity so captive-bred specimens are readily obtained.

Size: The size given is the average length of the full-grown lizards. Because of the considerable length of the tail in many species, the snout-vent length (SVL), measured from the snout to the cloacal vent, is also significant.

Terrarium size: The recommended terrarium dimensions indicate length × width × height (see page 11).

Feeding recommendations: The instructions apply to adult and adolescent animals.

Common House Gecko

Hemidactylus frenatus (see photo, page 12)

Length: 6 inches (14 cm). *Snout-vent length:* 3 inches (7 cm).

Distribution: Originally Southeast Asia, but has spread to almost all tropical continents.

10 Acquiring a Lizard and Getting It Settled

Habitat: Woods, thickets, cultivated land, human settlements.
Behavior: Active by night; gregarious.
Care: Woodland terrarium, 24 × 16 × 20 inches (60 × 40 × 50 cm).
Decorations: Branches and bark in the background; they should be removable because the gecko's eggs will be attached and must be easily transferred to the incubator.
Temperature: By day 73–86°F (23–30°C); by night 68–77°F (20–25°C).
Humidity: 70–90 percent.
Diet: Three times a week; insects and spiders, baby mice as a treat.
Special notes: Slit pupil. Adhesive lamellae do not reach to tips of toes, so the genus is also called the "half-finger gecko."

Golddust Day Gecko

Phelsuma laticauda (see photo, page 56)
Length: 5 inches (12 cm). *Snout-vent length:* 2 inches (6 cm).
Distribution: Eastern Madagascar, Comoro Islands. *Habitat:* Woods, thickets, cultivated land, human settlements.
Behavior: Active by day; lives in trees.
Care: Woodland terrarium, 24 × 16 × 20 inches (60 × 40 × 50 cm).
Decorations: Branches and plenty of plants.
Temperature: By day 79–86°F (26–30°C); by night 64–73°F (18–23°C); sunning areas and UV light.
Humidity: 50–70 percent.
Diet: Three times a week; insects and spiders.
Special notes: Adhesive lamellae; pupils without slits.
Species requiring similar care: Striped day gecko, *Phelsuma lineata,* 5 inches (12 cm), snout-vent length 2 inches (6 cm); Madagascar.
Green anole, *Anolis carolinensis,* 8 inches (20 cm), snout-vent length 3 inches (7 cm); southeastern North America.
Brown anole, *Anolis sagrei* (see page 48); 8 inches (20 cm), snout-vent length 3 inches (7 cm); Bahamas, Greater Antilles, southeastern North America, Central America.

Madagascar Day Gecko

Phelsuma madagascariensis (see photo, page 13)
Length: 10 inches (25 cm). *Snout-vent length:* 5 inches (13 cm).

Collared lizards, spiny lizards, and curlytail lizards can also be housed together, if they are the same size.

Species Profiles

Distribution: Madagascar, Seychelles. *Habitat:* Woods, thickets, cultivated land, human settlements.
Behavior: Active by day; lives in trees and on leaves; gregarious.
Care: Woodland terrarium, 48 × 24 × 40 inches (120 × 60 × 100 cm).
Decorations: Branches and plenty of plants.
Temperature: By day 79–86°F (26–30°C); by night 64–73°F (18–23°C); sunning areas and UV light.
Humidity: 60–80 percent.
Diet: Three times a week; insects and spiders.
Special notes: Adhesive lamellae; pupils without slits.
Species requiring similar care: Knight anole, *Anolis equestris* (see page 38); 16 inches (40 cm), snout-vent length 7 inches (17 cm); Cuba, southeastern North America; slightly greater humidity.

Fat-tail Gecko

Hemitheconyx caudicinctus (see photo, page 12)
Length: 8 inches (20 cm). *Snout-vent length:* 5 inches (12 cm).
Distribution: Western Africa. *Habitat:* Arid regions.
Behavior: Active by night; ground dwelling; gregarious. During the day, the geckos seek out cool damp caves, which they inhabit commonly.

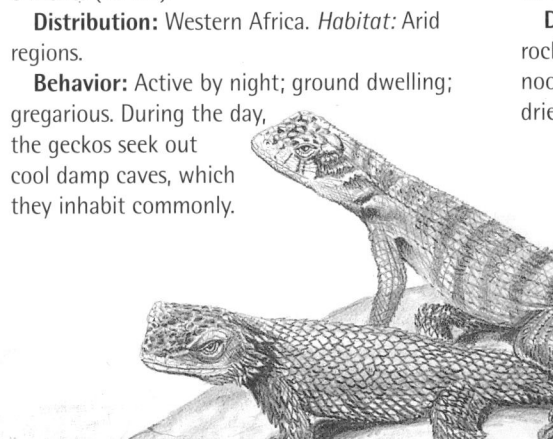

TIP

Terrarium Size

The terrarium sizes listed in the species profiles are based on standard guidelines for keeping reptiles. The sizes are based on the body length of fully-grown lizards as listed here, not the maximum length reached by occasional specimens. The sizes are calculated from the snout-vent length and allow for two lizards in the terrarium. For each additional animal, increase the terrarium volume by at least 15 percent. If the lizards are only half this size, the dimensions may be reduced by half—but a larger terrarium would do no harm.

Care: Desert terrarium, 24 × 20 × 20 inches (60 × 50 × 50 cm).
Decorations: Rock piles, sand, rock debris providing damp nooks and crannies, dried grasses.

12 PROFILES: LIZARDS

Common house gecko

Collared lizard

Fat-tail gecko

Temperature: By day 86°F (30°C); by night 68°F (20°C); during the winter rest from November to February, constant temperature of about 68°F (20°C).

Humidity: 50–70 percent.

Diet: Three times a week; insects and baby mice.

Special notes: No adhesive lamellae.

Species requiring similar care: Leopard gecko, *Eublepharis macularius* (see page 57, juvenile on page 16); 8 inches (20 cm), snout-vent length 5 inches (12 cm); Asia Minor, northwestern India.

Banded gecko, *Coleonyx variegatus* (see drawing, page 22 top left), 6 inches (14 cm), snout-vent length 3 inches (7 cm); southwestern North America, northern Central America.

Sailfin lizard

Veiled Chameleon

Chamaeleo calyptratus (see photo, page 17)

Length: 22 inches (55 cm). *Snout-vent length:* 10 inches (25 cm).

Distribution: southwestern Arabian Peninsula. *Habitat:* Thickets, at higher altitudes also in rare fringing forests.

Behavior: Active by day; lives in the branches of bushes and trees.

Inland bearded dragons

Water dragon

Madagascar day gecko

Spiny lizards

Diet: Three times a week; insects, an occasional baby mouse; blossoms, and chopped romaine.

Green Spiny Lizard
Sceloporus malachiticus (see photo, page 53)
  Length: 8 inches (20 cm). *Snout-vent length:* 3 inches (8 cm).
  Distribution: Central America. *Habitat:* In mountains to 4,900 feet (1,500 m), light woods.

  Care: Woodland terrarium, 60 × 24 × 40 inches (150 × 60 × 100 cm).
  Decorations: Branches just thick enough that they can be grasped with the toes; tough-leafed plants.
  Temperature: By day 77–90°F (25–32°C); by night 59–64°F (15–18°C); provide sunning areas and UV light.
  Humidity: 60–95 percent.

Acquiring a Lizard and Getting It Settled

Behavior: Active by day; inhabits ground and tree trunks; gregarious; ovoviviparous.
Care: Dry forest terrarium, 24 × 16 × 16 inches (60 × 40 × 40 cm).
Decorations: Stones, stumps, sand or sandy soil, not completely dry; tough-leafed plants.
Temperature: By day up to 95°F (35°C) in some spots, and lizards must have access to cooler places; by night 59°F (15°C); during the winter rest from November to February, 59–69°F (15–20°C); sunning areas and UV light; sun terrarium.
Humidity: 50–80 percent.
Diet: Three times a week; insects, baby mice, occasionally leaves and flowers.
Species requiring similar care: Crevice spiny lizard, *Sceloporus poinsettii* (see pages 6–7); 10 inches (25 cm), snout-vent length 5 inches (12 cm); arid regions, southwestern North America, northern Central America; provide drier climatic conditions.

Collared Lizard

Crotaphytus collaris (see photo, page 12)
Length: 12 inches (30 cm). *Snout-vent length:* 4 inches (10 cm).
Distribution: southwestern North America, northern Central America. *Habitat:* Rocky arid regions.
Behavior: Active by day; lives on ground and among rocks; gregarious.
Care: Desert terrarium, 24 × 20 × 20 inches (60 × 50 × 50 cm).
Decorations: Rock piles, sand, rock debris, dried shrubs.
Temperature: By day up to 113°F (45°C) in some spots, and lizards must have access to cooler places; by night 59°F (15°C); during the winter rest from November to February, 50–59°F (10–15°C); sunning areas and UV light.
Humidity: 50–70 percent.
Diet: Three times a week; insects, baby mice, other lizards; also leaves and flowers.
Species requiring similar care: Can be kept only with lizards larger than Collared. **Haitian curlytail lizard,** *Leiocephalus personatus* (see pages 42–43); 10 inches (25 cm), snout-vent length 5 inches (12 cm); Cuba, Bahamas.

The spiny-tailed agamid lives in hot deserts on rocks and rock debris.

Green Iguana

Iguana iguana (see photo, page 8)

Length: 60 inches (150 cm). *Snout-vent length:* 20 inches (50 cm).

Distribution: Mid-Central America to mid-South America. *Habitat:* Tropical rain forests and savanna trees, always in the immediate vicinity of water.

Behavior: Active by day; tree-dwelling; gregarious, but only one adult male per group. Likes to swim.

Care: Forest terrarium, 100 × 60 × 80 inches (250 × 150 × 200 cm).

Decorations: Branches for climbing, at least as thick in diameter as the lizard's torso. Water basins. Floor surface dampened for humidity.

Temperature: By day 77–95°F (25–35°C); by night 68–72°F (20–22°C); sunning areas and UV light; sun terrarium.

Humidity: 60–90 percent.

Diet: Daily; primarily vegetarian. Juveniles and some adults also eat large insects, earthworms, and fish, but this should be limited to 5 percent of the total diet. The vegetarian portion (greens, grasses, fruit, carrots, rice) increases as the animals grow. Provide adequate amounts of vitamin and mineral supplements during the growth period (see *Metabolic Bone Disease* and *Convulsive Trembling*, page 56).

Special notes: Long, sharp claws; whiplike tail.

Species requiring similar care: Sailfin lizard, *Hydrosaurus amboinensis* (see page 12); 40 inches (100 cm), snout-vent length 12 inches (30 cm); Southeast Asia.

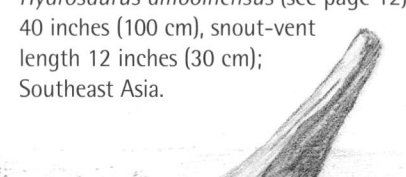

TIP

Species Conservation

The Washington Convention on International Trade in Endangered Species (CITES) of Wild Fauna and Flora provides for the protection of flora and fauna whose worldwide survival is threatened. Depending on how much protection is needed, various species of reptiles, including lizards, are listed in categories I or II. Animals threatened with extinction are listed in Appendix I. These animals may not be sold or bought without special permission. Other reptiles are listed under CITES in Appendix II. Being placed on one of the CITES appendices only means that permits are needed before the animals can be imported into the United States; CITES does not affect the sale or transport of animals within the United States.

Many states protect their native reptiles, forbidding harassment or removal from the wild and prohibiting private possession, commercial trade, or barter in the protected species. The Federal Endangered Species Act enforces state protection by prohibiting interstate transport, trade, or barter in any protected species.

All of the lizards described in the species profiles in this book can be kept in captivity, bred, and sold or bartered according to current regulations. Be aware that individual states may change their regulations for individual species of reptiles from time to time. Keep up to date on current regulations and laws by consulting magazines for reptile fanciers or by checking with appropriate authorities.

16 PROFILES: LIZARDS

Leopard gecko, juvenile coloration

Ridgetail monitor

Water Dragon
Physignathus concincinus (see photo, page 13)
Length: 32 inches (80 cm). *Snout-vent length:* 10 inches (25 cm).
Distribution: Indochina. *Habitat:* Tropical rain forest, always in immediate vicinity of water.
Behavior: Active by day; tree-dwelling; gregarious. A special feature is the lizard's flight behavior; when danger threatens, it jumps into the water and dives out of sight. Frequently has a damaged nose as a result.
Care: Rain forest terrarium, 60 × 32 × 40 inches (150 × 80 × 100 cm).
Decorations: Branches for climbing; large water basin; tough-leafed plants.

Mountain horned dragon

Temperature: By day 77–86°F (25–30°C); by night 68–77°F (20–25°C).
Humidity: 80–90 percent.
Diet: Three times a week; insects, earthworms, freshwater fish, baby rats and mice; some water dragons also like vegetables such as carrots.

Solomon Island skink

Veiled chameleon

Lined gecko

Spotted tree monitor

Common basilisk, *Basiliscus basiliscus* (see pages 1–2), 32 inches (80 cm), snout-vent length 10 inches (25 cm), southern Central America, northwestern South America.

Mountain Horned Dragon

Acanthosaura crucigera (see photo, page 16)

Length: 10 inches (24 cm). *Snout-vent length:* 4 inches (9 cm).

Distribution: Indochina, Malay peninsula. *Habitat:* Fog-dampened mountain forests and tea plantations up to elevations of 2,600 feet (800 m).

Species requiring similar care: Eastern water dragon, *Physignathus lesueurii* (see page 20); 36 inches (90 cm), snout-vent length 12 inches (30 cm); western Australia.

Green basilisk, *Basiliscus plumifrons* (see pages 4–5), 28 inches (70 cm), snout-vent length 8 inches (20 cm); southern and mid-Central America.

Giant blue-tongued skink

Acquiring a Lizard and Getting It Settled

Behavior: Active by day; lives in trees and bushes; gregarious.
Care: Cool rain forest terrarium, 24 × 16 × 20 inches (60 × 40 × 50 cm).
Decorations: Branches, twigs, bark, plants.
Temperature: By day 68–77°F (20–25°C); by night 59–68°F (15–20°C); sunning areas and UV light.
Humidity: In the morning 100 percent (spray cool water early and then later turn on warming lamps); otherwise 70–90 percent.
Diet: Three times a week; insects and spiders.
Species requiring similar care: Mountain horned dragon, *Acanthosaura armata* (see drawing, below); 10 inches (26 cm), snout-vent length 4 inches (10 cm); Southeast Asia.
Lined gecko, *Gekko vittatus* (see page 17); 10 inches (25 cm); snout-vent length 6 inches (15 cm); Southeast Asia; active by night; slit pupil, adhesive lamellae.
Tokay gecko, *Gekko gekko* (see page 24), 14 inches (35 cm); snout-vent length 7 inches (18 cm); Southeast Asia; active by night; slit pupil, adhesive lamellae.

Spiny-tailed Agamid
Uromastix acanthinurus (see page 14)

Length: 16 inches (40 cm). *Snout-vent length:* 10 inches (25 cm).
Distribution: Northwestern Africa. *Habitat:* Rock-strewn fields, sandy deserts, savanna trees.
Behavior: Active by day; lives on ground; digs deep holes.
Care: Desert terrarium, 60 × 44 × 32 inches (150 × 110 × 80 cm). Somewhat delicate in captivity.
Decorations: Rock piles, sand, rock debris with damp nooks and crannies, and stumps.
Temperature: By day up to 104°F (40°C) in some spots, and lizards must have access to cooler places; by night 59°F (15°C); during the winter rest from November to February, 59–68°F (15–20°C); sunning areas and UV light.

The Mountain horned dragon (acanthosaurus armatus) comes from Southeast Asia.

Species Profiles

Which Lizards Can Live Together?

Compatible Species	Characteristics	Terrarium
Golddust day gecko, striped day gecko, green anole, brown anole	Active by day, live in trees	Forest terrarium with branches and plenty of plants
Green iguana, sailfin lizard, water dragon, green basilisk, common basilisk	Large, active by day, live in trees. May be very nervous	Rainforest terrarium with sturdy branches for climbing and water basin for bathing; for large iguanas, terrarium without plants
Spiny-tailed agamid, eastern blue-tongued skink, giant blue-tongued skink, inland bearded dragon	Active by day, live on the ground	Desert terrarium with rock piles, sand, rock debris, stumps, and damp nooks and crannies to crawl into
Haitian curlytail lizard, northern curlytail lizard	Active by day, live on the ground	Desert terrarium with rock piles, sand, rock debris, and dry grasses
Leopard gecko, western banded gecko	Active by night, live on the ground	Desert terrarium with rock piles, sand, rock debris, and damp nooks and crannies to crawl into

The table lists species that can be kept together in the same terrarium. For general tips on housing lizards together, please see page 50.

Humidity: 50–70 percent.
Diet: Daily; vegetable fare, rarely insects or baby mice.
Species requiring similar care: Eastern blue-tongued skink, *Tiliqua scincoides*; 16 inches (40 cm), snout-vent length 12 inches (30 cm); northern and western Australia; ovoviviparous; also eats meat.
Giant blue-tongued skink, *Tiliqua gigas* (see page 17); 22 inches (55 cm); snout-vent length 12 inches (30 cm); New Guinea; ovoviviparous; also eats meat.

Solomon Island Skink

Corucia zebrata (see photo, page 16)

Length: 26 inches (65 cm). *Snout-vent length:* 11 inches (28 cm).
Distribution: Solomon Islands. *Habitat:* Tropical rain forests and savanna trees.
Behavior: Active by day and in morning and evening twilight; lives in trees; ovoviviparous.
Care: Forest terrarium, 60 × 36 × 48 inches (150 × 90 × 120 cm).
Decorations: Branches for climbing, tough-leafed plants.
Temperature: By day 77–86°F (25–30°C); by night 68–77°F (20–25°C); during the winter rest from November to February, 59–68°F (15–20°C); sunning areas and UV light.

Acquiring a Lizard and Getting It Settled

Humidity: 70–90 percent.
Diet: Daily; leaves and flowers, rarely meat.
Species requiring similar care: Pink-tongued skink, *Hemisphaeriodon gerrardii* (see page 9); 16 inches (40 cm), snout-vent length 6 inches (15 cm); eastern Australia; eats meat, primarily snails.

Spotted Tree Monitor

Varanus timorensis (see photo, page 17)
Length: 24 inches (60 cm). *Snout-vent length:* 9 inches (22 cm).
Distribution: Timor, southern New Guinea. *Habitat:* Savanna trees.
Behavior: Active by day; lives on ground and in trees.

Eastern water dragons live in loose groups, and always with water close by. They feed largely on insects and other prey.

Care: Forest terrarium, 48 × 32 × 40 inches (120 × 80 × 100 cm).
Decorations: Branches for climbing, hiding places, tough-leafed plants.
Temperature: By day up to 95°F (35°C) in some spots; by night 68–77°F (20–25°C).
Humidity: 60–90 percent.
Diet: Three times a week; insects, mice, fish.
Species requiring similar care: Emerald monitor, *Varanus prasinus* (see drawing, page 23); 28 inches (70 cm), snout-vent length 10 inches (24 cm); New Guinea; tropical rain forests.

Selecting and Buying a Lizard

Ridgetail Monitor

Varanus acanthurus (see photo, page 16)
Length: 24 inches (60 cm). *Snout-vent length:* 9 inches (22 cm).
Distribution: Northern Australia. *Habitat:* Rock-strewn fields, savannas.
Behavior: Active by day; lives on ground; gregarious.
Care: Desert terrarium, 48 × 24 × 24 inches (120 × 60 × 60 cm).
Decorations: Rock piles, sand, stumps, hiding places.
Temperature: By day up to 104°F (40°C) in some spots, and lizards must have access to cooler places; by night 68°F (20°C); during the winter rest from November to February, 64–75°F (18–24°C); sunning areas and UV light.
Humidity: 50–70 percent.
Diet: Three times weekly; insects and mice.
Species requiring similar care: Inland bearded dragon, *Pogona vitticeps* (see page 13); 20 inches (50 cm), snout-vent length 9 inches (22 cm); northern and western Australia; eats meat and also vegetable fare.

Where to Get a Lizard

You can buy lizards in a pet store or from a breeder. Breeders will often offer lizards in herpetological magazines and newsletters (see page 62). The number of males and females will be represented by two numbers separated by a period: 1.2 means one male and two females.

Selecting the Right Lizard

Before buying, observe the animal:
✔ Ribs, vertebrae, and pelvic bones should not show too noticeably under the skin.
✔ Thighs and the root of the tail should look muscular.
✔ The eyes should not lie too deep in the head.
✔ Check for external parasites.

Checklist
Buying a Lizard

1 Learn all you can ahead of time, so that you can make an informed selection. Spur-of-the-moment purchases are often costly.

2 A responsible seller will give you plenty of advice. Compare this advice carefully with the information you have gathered.

3 Inspect the lizard's living quarters. If the terrarium facilities are not clean and well maintained, the lizard may carry diseases that are not otherwise evident.

4 Take plenty of time to observe the lizards before you choose. Only purchase animals that are in good condition.

5 Select lizards during their active period. A healthy lizard is wide-eyed and alert; if disturbed, it will flee or try to defend itself.

6 To minimize the time your new pet must spend in the transport container, have the quarantine terrarium ready for immediate occupancy.

HOW-TO: GETTING YOUR

Carrying Your Lizard Home

To carry your lizard home, place it in a cotton or muslin bag. In cool or cold weather, if the lizard is small, you can put it under your jacket to be warmed by your body heat. A large lizard will be put in its bag in a carton. In cool weather, the carton should be made of Styrofoam. If it is very cold, add a hot-water bottle to protect the lizard. Keep the temperature below 90°F (32°C) to prevent overheating.

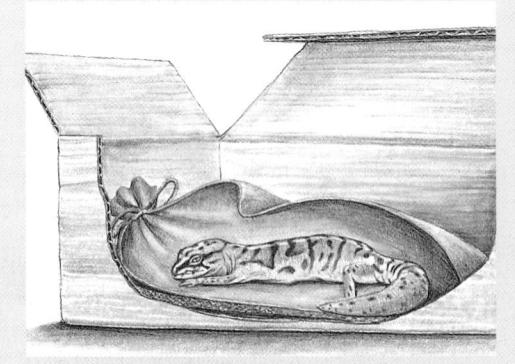

For safe transport, a lizard is packed in a bag and carton.

Getting Your Lizard Settled

Before you put your newly acquired pet in a terrarium that is inhabited by other lizards, it should spend some time in a quarantine terrarium. There the lizard can get used to its new surroundings without the stress of territorial disputes with other animals. Furthermore, this is the only possible way for you to monitor its behavior, food intake, and general health and to take the necessary stool samples (see page 55). The lizard should stay in quarantine quarters until it is free of parasites, healthy, and eating properly—at the minimum, for eight weeks.

Note: If your new lizard showed signs of ticks or mites when you bought it, administer the necessary treatment while it is still in the transport bag (see *Treating Illnesses*, page 54). Then place it in its quarantine quarters.

Insectivorous lizards have a better appetite if offered live prey.

First Feeding

Herbivorous lizards can be offered leaves or chopped fruit on the second day (see page 36).

Carnivorous lizards receive their first nourishment after a week. To stimulate their appetite, place live insects in the terrarium. Don't put in too much food at once, and remove any that remains uneaten after several hours.

An inland bearded dragon eyes a tempting morsel.

LIZARD SETTLED

The Quarantine Terrarium

Prepare the quarantine terrarium before you buy the lizard. An aquarium makes a quite suitable terrarium. As a rule of thumb for the size, you can use about half the dimensions given for your lizard species (see Species Profiles, pages 10–20). Cover the terrarium with a lid of fine wire screen on a sturdy frame. Side ventilation is usually not needed.

For ease of hygiene and handling, the setup should be simple and practical.

Lighting and heating: The terrarium must have a reflector lamp or heat lamp (see *Terrarium Technology,* pages 26–27). You will need to install additional floor heating only if it gets too cold at night.

Floor covering: Artificial turf is recommended, because it's easy to clean and disinfect. Besides, it serves some lizards as a cover. The humidity can be regulated if you dampen the absorbent mat as necessary. Artificial turf isn't suitable for basilisks and agamas because these lizards get their claws caught in it. You can use shredded newspaper for these.

Drinking-water container: This item can also serve as a bathing pool for those lizards that like to swim. Thus, it should be large enough that the lizard can fit its whole body into it.

Places to climb and hide: A sturdy branch in the terrarium gives tree-dwellers something to climb; a halved clay pipe or a curved piece of bark offers a hideaway for shy or nervous animals.

The quarantine terrarium must be simple and hygienic.

Note: If the lizard is especially uneasy, cover the front of the terrarium with a cloth or with paper. Leave the curtain in place until your pet has calmed down completely and then remove it gradually.

It's especially important at this time to offer a variety of food. Different colors and smells of vegetable food and the various movements of live food animals can whet your lizard's appetite. Take time to observe your pet as it settles in. This way you will learn how much food the lizard needs.

Quarantine Procedures
- ✔ Leave the lizard largely undisturbed.
- ✔ Change the drinking and bathing water.
- ✔ Remove and replace soiled paper and artificial turf.
- ✔ Remove feces; have feces samples tested.
- ✔ Monitor temperature and humidity.

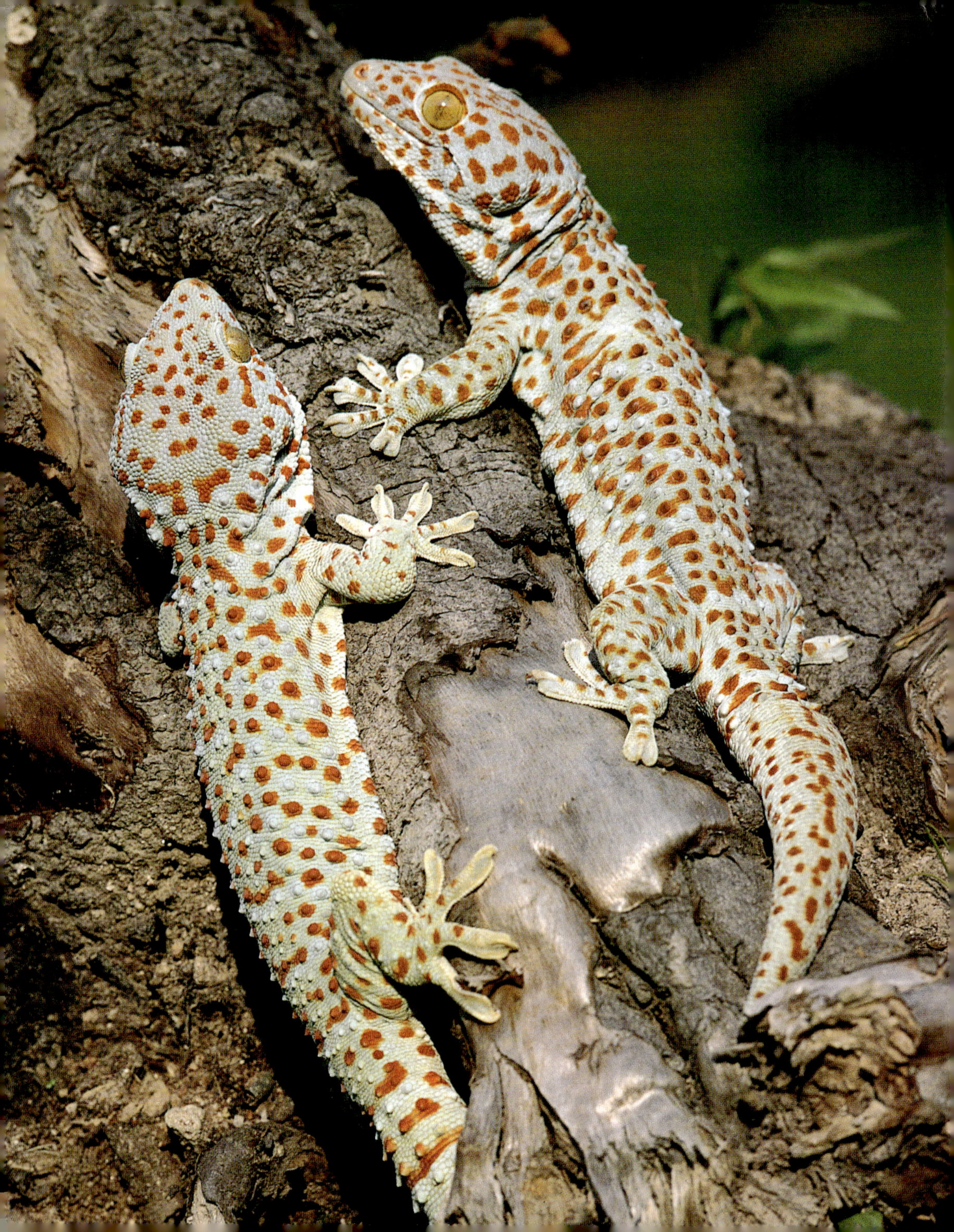

PROPER CARE AND FEEDING

The prerequisites for successful lizard-keeping are appropriate living space, the right food, and proper care. You must meet these essential needs if your lizards are to thrive, live a long life, and possibly even reproduce under your care.

The Terrarium

Pet stores offer terrariums in a wide variety of sizes and styles. Be sure to select a terrarium that is sturdily built and easy to clean and maintain.

Size: Lizards' space requirements depend not only on their size but above all on their behavior. Relatively small active species may require ample space to accommodate their territorial needs and demands. These animals establish territories and defend them. They suffer if the terrarium can't be divided into adequate territories. Other lizards, even if larger, need considerably less space because they are neither territorial nor free-ranging (see TIP, page 11).

Shape: Pet stores mostly carry the oblong, all-purpose terrariums, which generally have a length:width:height ratio of 2:1:1. These terrariums are primarily suitable for ground-dwelling species. Lizards that climb and live in trees or stone walls, on the other hand, need a terrarium that is twice as high as it is wide. Simply turn the terrarium up on its end.

Tokay geckos are active at night, and they do not always get along as well as these two.

Location: A terrarium may be free-standing or it can be built into a wall of shelves. If you are thinking of a built-in terrarium, you must consider beforehand how the terrarium can be heated, ventilated, and lighted without problems. Under no circumstances should a terrarium be exposed to direct sunlight, for it will quickly overheat and kill the animals within.

Ventilation

An important requirement for the successful care of lizards is fresh air. Nowhere—not even in the most stifling tropical jungle—is there so little movement of air as in a terrarium with solid sides. Therefore, at least 10 percent of the surface of both side and front walls must be perforated or made of wire screen; this air intake area must be located in the lower third of the walls, and at least an equal area of the terrarium roof must be made of wire screen as well. As the heat sources warm the air, it will rise and escape through the roof, drawing fresh air in from the sides. If the terrarium's structure or built-in location will not allow this ventilation system to work, you will need to install an aquarium air pump or a rotary or tangential fan.

Proper Care and Feeding

Terrarium Technology

To create a suitable living space for lizards, you must use electrical equipment such as heaters and lamps. Pet stores carry a variety of models.

Note: You must use caution when dealing with electrical equipment and wiring, which are especially dangerous when used in connection with water (see *Important Note*, page 63).

Heating

Reflector lamps: Many lizards are heliothermic, needing warmth and light; warmth by itself is not enough. Therefore, they need a heat source that gives light at the same time. For these animals you can install incandescent lamps. They are sold in stores as reflector spotlights. The wattage and the potential surface temperature you need depend on the requirements of the particular type of lizard (see Species Profiles, pages 10–20). Position the lights so water cannot be sprayed or splashed on the lamp.

Infrared lamps: For the less light-dependent lizards, such as most geckos, infrared lamps (60 to 250 watts) or ceramic heat bulbs can be installed for heat sources.

Note: Spotlights and heat lamps must be installed in such a way that the lizards can't reach them and get burned.

Bottom heating: At night, after the heat lamps are turned down, the temperature may fall below the minimum warmth the lizard needs (see Species Profiles, pages 10–20). If this is the case, you must install a source of bottom heat under at least one third of the terrarium area. You can buy heating cables, a heating mat, or electrically heated rocks.

Gentle floor heating is also recommended if the necessary degree of humidity can't be maintained by frequent spraying of the plants. You can then spray the floor, and evaporation of the dampness will produce the proper humidity.

Note: Follow carefully the instructions for installing the heat source. Only heating cables with low surface temperatures should be used. Cover the heating cable or mat with wire mesh made of stainless steel to protect it from damage if the lizards dig in the ground.

Lighting

Lizards of tropical species that are active by day will be comfortable only if there is enough bright light. Because plants and animals have different light requirements, the position of the lights within a terrarium must supply the needs of the plants and animals.

Fluorescent lamps are suitable for terrariums up to 28 inches (70 cm) in height. They are inexpensive and economical in use of power. Such lamps produce satisfactory plant growth, and the color of both plants and animals will appear natural. But fluorescent lamps give off hardly any heat.

Spotlights are excellent sources of localized warmth and light. The ideal is a combination of fluorescent lamps and spotlights. Use the spotlights to create "sunning spots," away from plants, where a lizard can come to bask.

Mercury vapor and halogen vapor lamps are only recommended for very large terrariums [at least 1.4 cubic yards (1 m^3) in volume]. They give off so much light and heat that to protect the plants and animals, the lamps must be located outside the terrarium and at least 40 inches (1 m) away from its contents. They are rarely used in the United States and are difficult to obtain.

Ultraviolet (UV) lights stimulate biological processes. Essential for lizards are UV-B rays, which control calcium metabolism, and UV-A rays, which are very important for pigment formation in the skin. These are available in bulbs that fit an ordinary aquarium reflector and can be safely used as part of the normal day/night cycle.

Note: A period for getting used to intense UV radiation is absolutely necessary. Begin with an exposure of one minute only and lengthen the time daily, until after two months a time span of one hour has been reached.

Temperature and Humidity

The daily and seasonal variations of temperature and humidity in the lizard's natural habitat must be simulated artificially in the terrarium (see *Climate Control*, page 34).

✔ To control the day-night rhythm, the terrarium's heating and lighting systems are connected to a timer. If you are away from home during the day, you can adjust the timing so that you can still observe your lizard's normal daytime activities in the evening.

✔ To monitor and control temperature changes, use a thermostat with timer. Install the thermostat in a safe place, out of reach of the lizards. Of course, the thermostat should not be in the direct path of light from a warming lamp.

✔ Because thermostats wear out with use and can fail, you should also monitor the temperature in the terrarium with a thermometer. A simple indoor thermometer is just as satisfactory as a battery-operated digital thermometer. A thermometer that indicates daily minimum and maximum temperatures is very useful.

✔ The degree of relative humidity is measured with a hygrometer.

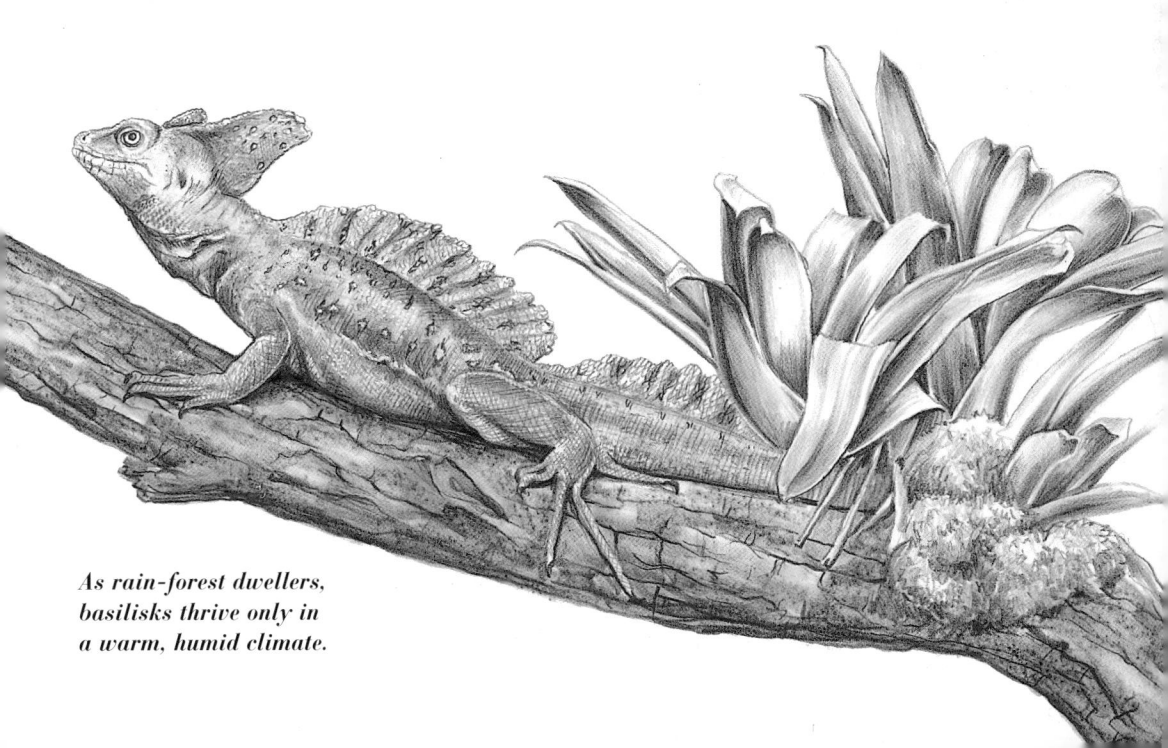

As rain-forest dwellers, basilisks thrive only in a warm, humid climate.

Plants in the Terrarium

Terrarium plants are not just for decoration. They also influence the microclimate, provide the lizards with cover, and create a visual screen, thus establishing the individual territories many types of lizards need.

Choosing the Right Plants

It isn't necessary for the lizards' well-being that the plants come from the same area that they do. But many terrarium enthusiasts find it fun to create geographical unity between animals and planting. You can choose from a wide variety of desert plants and rainforest plants (see page 32). Make sure when you buy terrarium plants that they are robust enough for your lizards. Will they survive a leap, for instance, or tightly clinging sharp claws? Hard-leafed, dark green plants are generally less delicate than those with tender, bright green, or colored foliage.

Plant Care

Lighting: Plants need light. It is essential for the production of chlorophyll, which in turn is necessary for plant vigor. If too little light is available, the plant will grow toward what light there is, producing longer and thinner shoots. If your plants show signs of lack of light, remove them from the terrarium and place them in a bright location until they recover. Fluorescent lamps can provide sufficient light levels for plants to thrive (see page 26).

Planting medium: A good planting medium for terrarium plants is leaf mold or decayed pine needles. If the depth is more than 2 inches (5 cm), provide a drainage layer of gravel or broken clay pots.

Epiphytes (air plants): Typical of tropical rainforests, these plants rest on branches of other plants. To plant:

✔ Free the hold fast of any dry soil.
✔ Pack it in sphagnum moss, coconut fiber, fern roots, or other plant material that drains readily, and press it into the fork of an epiphyte support or tie or staple it to a branch.
✔ Air plants can also be stuck in a suitably large hole in a branch or in a crack.
✔ Take care that any water can run off; epiphytes grow this way to avoid standing water. You may need to bore a small hole through the support branch.

Watering: For watering, use only clean rainwater or salt-free water that you can buy or produce yourself with an ion exchanger (pet store). The water temperature should be the same as the terrarium temperature. It's easier to control the amount if you use a plant mister rather than a watering can.

Plant pests: Sprays or insecticides must not be used in the terrarium. Try to wipe away leaf aphids and scale with a soft damp cloth or sponge. Also increase the humidity, because these insects thrive in a setting that is too dry.

Changing plants: Plants that get too little light or are infested by stubborn pests must be removed from the terrarium. To make removal easier, leave the plants in pots; sink the pots into the floor material deeply enough that the tops don't show.

Desert Plants

The maintenance of plants from dry areas often turns out to be difficult because the humidity in the terrarium is usually too high and light levels too low for them. Expect to change them more often so that they can recover.

Pincushion cactus *(Mammillaria):* Several varieties available; size varies; like other cacti, may bloom in winter if given light and cool dry conditions.

Suitable Plants for the Terrarium

Bromeliads are typical rainforest plants (see page 32).

A spiderwort in bloom is a special treat (see page 32).

Opuntia *(Opuntia):* Many varieties available; size varies; avoid varieties with especially long spines.

Bowstring hemp *(Sansevieria):* Available in various types and sizes; needs more water than jade plants do.

Jade plants *(Crassula falcata, Crassula portulacea):* Should be changed frequently because the plants grow rapidly.

Euphorbia *(Euphorbia):* Many varieties and various sizes available; low-growing (see photo, page 32).

Aloe, gasteria, haworthia *(Aloe, Gasteria, Haworthia):* Available in many varieties; uncomplicated maintenance; well suited to small terrariums, because they remain small.

HOW-TO: HOUSING

The Desert Terrarium

The stark beauty of a desert habitat can be recreated in the terrarium with sand, stones, and dried wood.

Rock piles: The individual stones must be glued together, and the pile must be firmly fastened directly to the terrarium floor. If you simply pile rocks on the sand, the lizards can tunnel under them, tip them over, and be injured. Use a clear silicone caulk that is safe to use in aquariums. Pet stores also sell artificial rock structures.

Display spots and hiding places: Rock piles and climbing branches serve not only as display places for dominant lizards, but as sunning spots for all. Be sure to locate them where the beams from the warming lamps will shine on them. Also provide plenty of hiding places—crannies among rocks and roots, or simple half-cylinders of clay, wood, or cork. Mist the floors of these nooks daily, so your lizard will have cool, damp hiding places during the hot hours. The nooks and crannies should be large enough that a lizard can escape a pursuer, not be trapped inside. Also, you'll want to be able to see and reach inside.

Planting zones: If a desert terrarium has a floor area of at least 5.4 square feet (0.5 m^2), there will be room for some larger live plants (see page 29); install them where heat lamps and UV lamps won't burn them. Otherwise, choose small cacti, dried grasses, and plants for decoration.

The Rainforest Terrarium

The most noticeable features of a rainforest terrarium are the luxuriously growing plants (see page 32). They serve as decoration and at the same time provide hunting-ground boundaries for territorial lizards.

Arrangement of back and side walls:

✔ To install a plant wall, screening of plastic or stainless-steel wire [mesh size 0.25 to 0.50 inch (5–15 mm)] is mounted on a frame and glued to the terrarium wall with silicone caulk. Fill the space behind the mesh with peat moss and sphagnum. Then insert cuttings of vines or hanging plants directly into the substrate, fastening them with wire or plastic clips.

✔ Another suitable substrate for vines is compressed tree-fern "tiles" or slabs glued to the walls with silicone. After the adhesive dries, keep the walls moist.

✔ Walls masked with bark, bark planks, or bamboo provide the

Create an attractive desert scene with rocks and plantings.

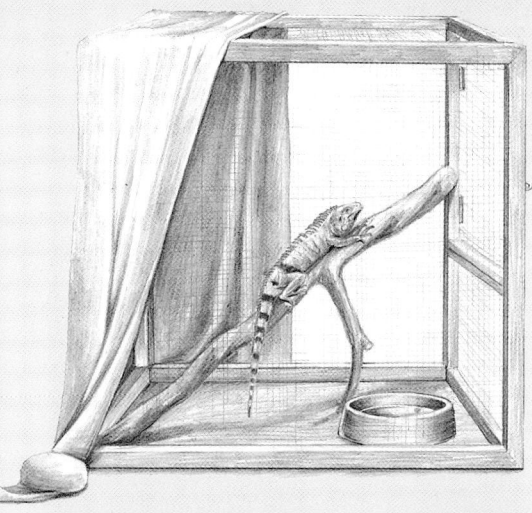

The Sun Terrarium

On warm sunny days, your lizards will enjoy a few hours in the fresh air. Build a sun terrarium with wood lath and wire mesh. It can be about half the size of the indoor terrarium. You must provide some shade and a good-sized bathing basin so your pet won't overheat.

Fresh air and sunshine that's not filtered through glass is good for a lizard's health.

ideal environment for species that live primarily on tree trunks. The coverings should not furnish any unreachable hiding places for lizards or for food animals.

Epiphytes and branches for climbing: Epiphytes (see page 28) are best supported on branches of hardwoods such as locust (*Robinia*), lilac (*Syringa*), and grape vines. Oak and the wood of stone-fruit trees (peaches, apricots, plums) are also good climbing branches. Cut the branches so that the cut surface will lie flat against the terrarium wall or floor, and fasten them with silicone caulk or screws to keep them from tipping or sliding. Otherwise, the lizards might get their tails caught.

Substrate: A one- (or at most two-) year-old leaf or pine-needle surface, which in larger terrariums is covered with fresh-fallen leaves, is ideal.

The ground-dwelling lizards can conceal themselves in this and, if they are not overfed, search in it for food.

Dense greenery in the rainforest terrarium offers many hiding places for lizards.

Water Containers

Desert terrarium: A small water basin, even a shallow pool in a natural stone setting, is often adequate.

Rainforest terrarium: Most lizards drink the water droplets that collect on the leaves of terrarium plants as you mist them. For species that like to swim, provide a bathing basin in which the largest resident lizard will have space to move freely.

Proper Care and Feeding

Rainforest Plants

Philodendrons *(Philodendron):* Available in many species and different sizes. Hanging and climbing plants with small to medium-size leaves; put out air roots.

Spathyphyllum *(Spathyphyllum):* Ground plants, occasionally with white blooms; the smaller forms are well suited to the terrarium.

Bromeliads *(Bromeliaceae):* Because of their typical growth habits and their usually epiphytical life style, they are best for creating small uncluttered landscapes (see photo, page 29).

✔ *Vriesea splendens,* a large variety with beautifully marked leaves, but there are forms available that remain small. Epiphytic; leaves grow in the form of a rosette, as do those of most bromeliads, forming a well in which water collects; many lizards use these as drinking places.

✔ *Tillandsia,* available in many varieties. These are typical epiphytes; grow partly without soil, only bound to wood; need much light and high nighttime humidity.

✔ *Aechmea, Guzmania* and *Nidularium,* many varieties and hybrids available. Various sizes, therefore suitable for many terrariums; epiphytic; sensitive to standing water.

✔ *Cryptanthus,* available in many varieties. Very decorative; grows mainly on the ground and only occasionally as an air plant.

Spiderwort *(Tradescantia):* Available in many varieties and forms; ground, hanging, and climbing plants (see photo, page 29).

Marantas *(Maranta, Calathea):* Herbaceous ground plants; suitable for larger terrariums; need light.

Aglaonema *(Aglaonema):* Available in many varieties and forms; herbaceous ground plants; must be cut back occasionally.

Spurge plants, native to Africa, will grow in desert terrariums (see page 28). Caution: toxic to humans and most animals.

Pothos *(Epipremnum pinnatum):* Ground, hanging, and climbing plants; thrives under relatively adverse conditions and reduced light; produces air roots.

Ficus *(Ficus benjamina):* Small-leaved ornamental fig; especially suitable for larger terrariums.

Sword fern *(Nephrolepsis exaltata):* Available in many forms. Ground plants; avoid standing water and floor heat.

Asparagus fern *(Asparagus):* Ground or hanging plants, available in many varieties; sensitive to standing water.

10 Golden Rules
for a Healthy Lizard

1 Lizards need no petting, but do need the lizard-keeper's critical attention.

2 Routine care and hygiene are essential not only for the lizard's health, but also for your own protection.

3 If all areas of the terrarium are readily visible, it's much easier to do any chores and keep an eye on your pets.

4 Observe the lizards carefully and often, so you'll notice any changes in their behavior and appearance in time to respond.

5 Keep a log of what you observe. Your notes may be very useful if problems arise.

6 Try not to disturb the lizards with terrarium maintenance. Except for the necessary cleaning, leave your pets in peace.

7 Any disruption causes stress to the lizards, although they may become less shy as they grow used to you.

8 Remove feces daily; as you do so, check its consistency. If there is feces and urine in the water container, change the water completely; otherwise, simply replenish it.

9 Use only clean rainwater or salt-free water to mist the terrarium plants.

10 Always close the terrarium securely. Escaped lizards have little chance of survival. What's more, they may frighten the people they encounter.

Proper Care and Feeding

Basic Terrarium Maintenance

To give your lizards the best living conditions, you will need to clean and maintain the terrarium on a regular basis. The lizards can stay in the terrarium as you do routine daily tasks. For more extensive procedures, such as replacing plants and other fixtures, move the lizards to another terrarium while you work.

Note: Always wash your hands thoroughly after working in the terrarium and handling the lizards.

Climate Control

Because lizards cannot produce their own warmth, they are dependent on the correct temperature in their terrarium to function. In addition to temperature, however, climate includes humidity, light, seasonal changes, and the rhythm of day and night. This means that the lizard-keeper must constantly monitor and adjust these factors (see *Terrarium Technology*, pages 26–27).

Temperature control: This is especially vital in those terrarium locations where the temperature may be influenced by external factors, such as direct sunlight.

Humidity control: Humidity is of particular importance for lizards from extreme humidity zones. This is equally true for lizards from tropical mountain forests, where the nights are cool and damp, and for lizards from desert regions, where the nighttime cooling generates a relative humidity of 100 percent for a brief time. Both produce condensed droplets for drinking. The necessary humidity is achieved by spraying the plants daily or by moistening a gently heated floor medium.

Cleaning the Terrarium

✔ With a simple arrangement of decorations, you will be able to complete cleaning tasks quickly and thoroughly.
✔ Cleaning implements such as sponges, brushes, scoops, and tweezers must be washed thoroughly in hot water after each use. Disinfect them at regular intervals.
✔ For hygienic and aesthetic reasons, remove feces and urine daily.
✔ The floor medium will need to be renewed occasionally to prevent bad odors.
✔ Remove the lizards during this procedure.

Trim the claws as indicated by the straight lines.

Care of Several Terrariums

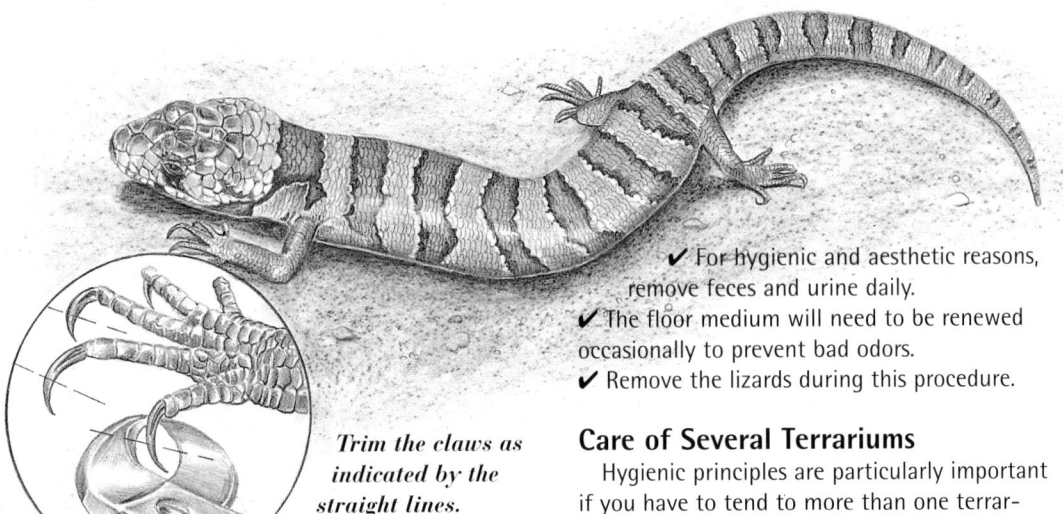

Hygienic principles are particularly important if you have to tend to more than one terrarium. To rule out the danger of an infection or the transfer of a parasite infestation, observe the following procedures:

✔ Use a separate set of cleaning tools for each terrarium. Disinfect them well after each use.

✔ Food remnants or food animals not eaten by the lizards in one terrarium must never be used to feed lizards in another terrarium.

✔ When setting up or renewing terrarium arrangements, disinfect containers and equipment thoroughly. Use new decorations.

Changing the Water

If the water in drinking and bathing containers is contaminated with feces or food residues, change it at once. Fresh water for the bathing basin should be at the accustomed temperature.

Grooming

In some circumstances you will need to assist lizards with their body care.

Skin remnants: Most lizards molt without any difficulty. In rare cases—most often resulting from insufficient humidity—some skin will remain at the ends of the toes. If this skin dries out, it can constrict the toes so tightly that parts of them will be lost. To prevent this, soak the foot briefly in warm water or allow the lizard to run on damp bath toweling (see page 59). Then remove the skin. For lizards with adhesive lamellae on the undersides of their toes, a sign of molting problems is that they can no longer climb smooth surfaces. Soften and remove the dried skin as previously instructed for toe tips.

Trimming the claws: Climbing lizards need long, sharp claws. Ground-dwelling lizards whose claws do not wear down properly will need to have them clipped. Ask the veterinarian to teach you how to trim the claws.

VACATION CARE

Plan ahead to find a reliable person to care for your lizards while you're away—preferably someone already familiar with terrarium animals. To ease the duties, take the following steps:

✔ *Lower the temperature by about 9°F (5°C), for example by turning off the heating lamps and spots. Leave only the lighting needed for plants. This will induce a phase of decreased activity that considerably slows the lizards' metabolic processes. They will not need to be fed and the excrement will not collect as often as during conditions of optimum temperature. Watering, while still essential, will be less frequent.*

✔ *Tell your lizard-sitter that some temperature variation is normal. Clearly specify the maximum and minimum acceptable temperatures.*

✔ *The day before you leave, clean the terrarium thoroughly and stop feeding the lizards.*

✔ *If you are away for more than two weeks, the lizards should be fed.*

Proper Care and Feeding

A Healthy Diet

The eating habits of lizards vary as widely from species to species as do their habitats. Some lizards eat only animal prey, others live only on plants, and some eat both. The Species Profiles (pages 10-20) give details on what to feed lizards of a particular species.

Plants in the Diet

Grasses and weeds: For the plant-eating lizards, the most valuable foods are wild grasses and weeds (such as dandelion, plantain, clover, and chickweed). You can gather the greens yourself, but avoid areas along high-traffic roads where the plants are heavily exposed to pollutants.

Fruit and vegetables: Also valuable are fruit and vegetables, from your own garden or elsewhere. Citrus fruits, sweet red peppers, carrots, spinach, and kale are high in needed vitamins. Wash before chopping and serving to remove surface pesticides.

Rice mixtures: In winter, when fresh food is more scarce, you can feed cooked brown rice mixed with minced bananas, apples, or unsulfured raisins. To promote digestion, mix in a little hay, chopped in pieces 1/4-inch to 2 inches (0.5–5 cm) long, depending on the size of the lizard. To avoid deficiency diseases, enrich the rice-and-fruit mixture with vitamin and mineral supplements (see page 37).

Insects in the Diet

Lizards that eat insect prey should have the opportunity to hunt down live insect food. Lizards that eat mice, rats, or birds can be trained to eat pre-killed prey. All these animals can be purchased frozen and then thawed before using. Store-bought meat, such as ground beef, is not suitable for these lizards. They need to ingest the skeleton, hair, scales, chitin, and stomach contents of their prey, not only for the vitamins and minerals these provide, but also to keep their digestive tracts healthy.

Note: Food insects and animals are sold in pet stores. There are also farms that specialize in raising insects and rodents; you can order what you need for delivery at regular intervals.

Insects, spiders, small mammals:
✔ Larger lizards relish mice and grasshoppers.
✔ Crickets are suitable for many species of lizards.
✔ Cockroaches are acceptable but they are escape artists.
✔ Aphids and fruit flies are ideal food for young lizards. In summer, you can lure the flies with fruit.
✔ Crickets and spiders can be ordered through a pet shop or caught with a net in a meadow or a weedy vacant lot. Be aware that you may not net insects in certain protected areas, and your catch must not include any protected species.

Note: Conservation groups or state authorities can provide information regarding conservation regulations.

Freshwater fish: Never offer fish filleted—only whole (with scales, bones, entrails, stomach contents, and all) to ensure a good supply of minerals and vitamins.

Snails and worms: In damp weather you can collect slugs and small snails. These mollusks can be kept in a closed container, sufficiently large and with air holes in it, in a cool room or in a refrigerator for three to four weeks. The edible snails sold in gourmet food shops are another option. You can buy earthworms in a bait shop, dig them from your garden or compost heap, collect them on warm rainy days, or buy them through classified ads in fishing magazines.

A Healthy Diet

Vitamins and Minerals

Vitamins are essential for normal growth and activity. They are ingested with the food or formed during the digestive process. Sunlight or UV light is usually needed for the formation/metabolization of vitamin D3.

Minerals like calcium, phosphorus, and magnesium are primarily needed for the development of bones and teeth. Therefore, it's especially important for young and growing animals to have a good supply of minerals.

Trace elements such as potassium, iron, iodine, fluorine, and selenium are important for the formation of enzymes and hormones.

Vitamin and mineral supplements: To meet the nutritional needs of terrarium-dwelling lizards, vitamin and mineral supplements must

The green basilisk can scamper right across the surface of the water.

be added to the food or to the drinking water. If signs of deficiency are observed (see pages 54–59), it may also be necessary to give supplements directly.

Vitamin and mineral supplements are available as drops or powder from pet stores, pharmacies, or the veterinarian, who can also advise you about the right dose. Drops are placed directly in the lizard's mouth; powder is mixed with the food. Give only as directed.

Note: Another good source of minerals is available in crushed eggshells or cuttlebone, sprinkled on the food once a week.

HOW-TO: FEEDING

Feeding Times

Lizards that are active by day are fed during the day or during the day phase established by a timer (see page 27). Nocturnal lizards receive their food toward the evening.

Feeding Herbivorous Lizards

Rice and diced fruit and vegetables are offered in a bowl; greens, grasses, and leafy vegetables can be placed on the floor of the terrarium. If there are several lizards, you should place the greens in different places so that the lower-ranking animals will get their share.

During the winter months, supplement fresh foods with rice and a vitamin-mineral preparation.

Becasue supplements change the appearance, odor, and taste of the food, you must accustom the lizards to them by gradually increasing the amount.

A tame young knight anole swallows an insect.

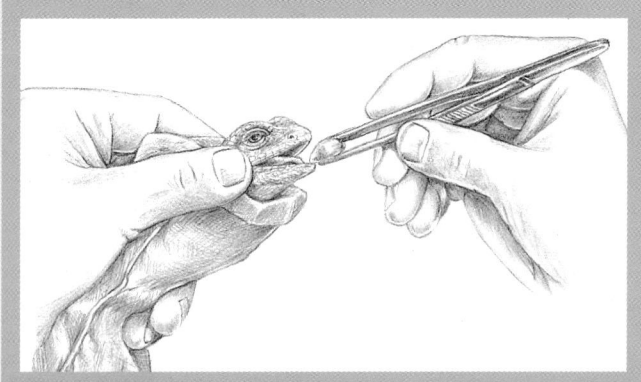

If force-feeding is necessary, hold the lizard gently and introduce the food carefully.

Force-feeding

A lizard that has refused food for a long time may need to be force-fed. Before taking such drastic measures, however, you should definitely consult a person experienced in the care of lizards.

To force-feed a small lizard, hold it in one hand and open its mouth with the other (see drawing). For a larger lizard, you will need someone to help you. It's best to place the lizard's body in a cotton sack to protect yourself against its sharp claws. While one person holds the lizard (see page 54), the other opens its mouth. If there is a dewlap or enough skin in the under jaw, the lizard may be grasped there and the mouth opened with a steady pull. To keep the mouth open, press firmly at the corners or insert a firm roll of cotton, the type your dentist uses.

Feeding Carnivorous Lizards

Slugs and small snails with shells may be put into the terrarium alive in small quantities. The lizards like to crack open the shells.

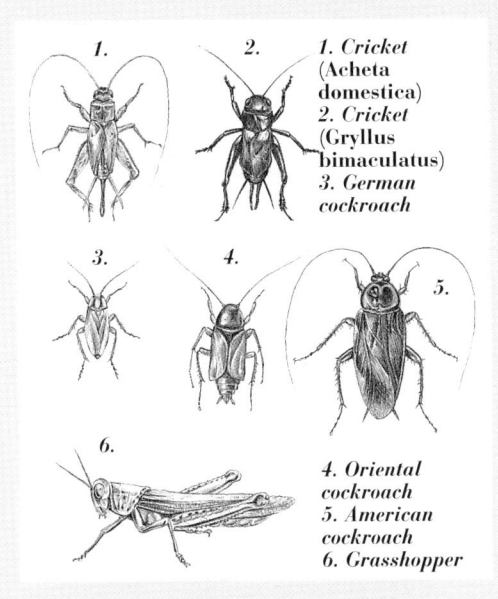

1. Cricket (Acheta domestica)
2. Cricket (Gryllus bimaculatus)
3. German cockroach
4. Oriental cockroach
5. American cockroach
6. Grasshopper

Large edible snails should be scalded, removed from the shell, and cut up before being fed to lizards.

Aphids can be placed in the terrarium; simply place them on twigs and leaves, and put them in the terrarium.

Live insects should be given to the lizards one at a time to be sure they're eaten as soon as possible. If they escape, you'll hear them chirping at night, and they can eat the plants and even bite the lizards. To avoid this, the lizard may be trained to receive the live insect directly from tweezers.

Small mammals and fish should be killed and offered with tweezers.

Note: Animals that have been removed from the freezer must be thawed completely before feeding so that they reach room temperature all the way through. Thaw in warm water and blot dry.

Many lizards satisfy their need for water by licking droplets from foliage.

Food supplements: One method is to put a pinch of the powdered supplement in a plastic bag or other container, then add the live insects and shake vigorously to coat the insects with powder. Feed them at once so they can't shake the powder off. For large lizards, the vitamin and mineral supplements can be placed in the abdominal cavities of dead mice or fish. Smaller lizards that ingest their drinking water drop-by-drop can receive their vitamins in the drinking water.

Don't try to force dietary supplements into healthy lizards. The stress of being caught and force-fed can do more harm than the vitamin and mineral intake would do good.

Water for Lizards

Rainforest terrarium: Mist the plants daily with water; the lizards will lick the droplets from the leaves. Additional water in the drinking dish and bathing basin should be changed three times a week, unless it is soiled. Then change it immediately.

Desert terrarium: Mist with water early in the day, but only in parts of the terrarium. Provide a pool of drinking water and change it daily.

Proper Care and Feeding

Lizard Breeding

Successful breeding is reassurance that you have created optimal living conditions for your lizards. On the other hand, simply owning lizards that are well cared for does not guarantee successful breeding; the stimulation of sexual instinct is a critical component. Important factors can include the hours of daylight and the climate. In the areas near the equator, for example, the alternate dry and rainy seasons induce a resting phase (dry season) followed by the mating period (with the first rains of the wet season).

Therefore, it's essential that you know as much as possible about the origins of your lizards and their climate needs.

Courtship

Many forms of courtship are observable at mating time.
✔ Iguanas display their dewlap while nodding their heads.
✔ Agamas also nod their heads, and "wave" at the same time—that is, they execute a circular horizontal movement with a front leg. This is also used as an appeasement gesture.
✔ Male anoles woo a female with a quick nodding of the head and dewlap display.

The lizards may take almost no nourishment during the courtship period, in spite of their activity, but there is no cause for worry if they have been well nourished beforehand. Eating will follow later and often at an above-average rate for the female, who should be left alone after courtship has ended, because egg production demands an above-average supply of energy. Feed her heavily once the eggs have been laid or after the young have been born.

Mating

The sex organs of male reptiles are concealed within the cloaca. Male lizards possess paired organs called hemipenes which lie within sheaths in the ventral portion of the tail. For copulation, the male lizard approaches the female from the side. The males of many lizard species bite the neck of the female and try to maneuver the cloaca as close as possible to that of the female. The hemipenes are creased or grooved in a variety of species-specific ways and are provided with fleshy thorns or barbs that enable the lizards to cling together securely as they mate. With some reptiles, sperm can be stockpiled by the female so that fertilization of late-maturing eggs can still take place after months or years. The gestation period for the female varies from species to species.

Egg-Laying

As the day of egg-laying nears, the female will inspect the ground surface and dig holes in many places (see drawing, pages 42–43). She will continue to dig until one of these test holes meets with her approval; then egg-laying begins.

In most cases, the eggs must be transferred to an incubator. But this should not be done before the female has finished laying her eggs and has covered the nest hole again.

Young day geckos hatch from hard-shelled eggs.

Lizard Breeding 41

Any intervention too soon is a disturbance; the lizard may stop laying eggs and suffer laying distress.

Transferring the Eggs to the Incubator

An incubator is needed for brooding the eggs (incubation). Set it up during the mating period and have it ready. A discarded aquarium makes a good incubator. Install a heat source, controlled by a thermostat. The easiest way is to put 2–3 inches (5.25–6.8 cm) of water in the aquarium, and add a submersible aquarium heater. Add two bricks to rest the egg container upon. The temperature should be 79–86°F (26–30°C), that is, about the same temperature at which the lizards live. Before

During mating, the male Madagascar day gecko embraces the female (left) and grasps her about the neck (right).

transferring the eggs, you must be sure that the proper temperature has been reached.
✔ You need a clear, covered, plastic container for the clutch of eggs. Fill it 2.5–5 inches (6–12 cm) deep with vermiculite (mica that has been fired to become heat-resistant) from a pet or garden shop. Vermiculite comes in various grain sizes; the best mixture is vermiculite No. 3 VET mixed with water in proportions ranging from 1:1.5 to 1:1.2 parts by weight or 3 parts vermiculite to 1 part water by volume. The material

will retain this dampness in the almost closed container.

✔ After all the eggs are laid, carefully uncover the nest hole and remove the clutch. Unearthing must be done with special care because the eggs of most lizards have a flexible shell. You must also be careful to keep the eggs right side up, as found, while moving them. The embryo is fixed in the egg and may be smothered by the yolk supply if the position of the egg is changed.

✔ Settle the eggs in the box so they are covered with about ½ inch (1 cm) of incubating material. Close the box almost completely, so that a minimal amount of air circulation is still possible, and place it in the incubator.

✔ If you use vermiculite, the often-recommended inspection and removal of unfertilized eggs is not necessary.

The Young Lizard

The incubation time can vary widely from one lizard species to another. For monitors, it can last more than 200 days; for geckos, about 50 days. To free itself from the egg, the hatchling uses its egg tooth to slit open the shell. This is a tooth, located forward on the premaxillary bone, which grows in most lizard embryos and falls out a few days after hatching.

After hatching, the young lizards are placed in their own terrarium, arranged appropriately for the species of lizard, and kept under the same climatic conditions as the parents. There is no reason to keep them warmer. Any higher temperature—especially the failure to lower the temperature at night—does allow the young to grow more quickly, but the negative effects also show quickly. The calcium metabolism cannot keep pace, and rickets may develop (see page 56); vitamin B complex deficiencies may also lead to convulsive trembling (see page 56), and soon the promising offspring have become miserable objects of pity.

Live-Bearing Lizards

Not all lizards lay eggs; some species, such as skinks, give birth to live young. Embryo development occurs within the

The female Haitian curlytail lizard digs holes in several spots before laying her eggs. When she finds a test hole with the right temperature and humidity, she crawls into the hole and deposits her eggs. Then she scrapes the substrate back over the hole and tamps it down.

mother's body, albeit in a thin-skinned egg; therefore, for the most part, there is no connection to the circulation of the mother. There is another form of embryonic development in which nourishment is partially supplied by the mother's metabolism. In the ovoviviparous lizards, the young lizards hatch out of the egg membrane before, during, or immediately after the mother has laid the egg. These live-born young lizards should be raised in the terrarium in the same way as the incubator-hatched ones.

First Feeding

The time at which food is first taken can vary quite widely. Whereas skinks take their first food soon after birth, the reserves of some species can last for up to six weeks. You should not lose patience and resort to force-feeding. This will cause the young lizards stress, which endangers their general health and future hardiness.

Food for young lizards must be rich in variety. Give particular attention to the calcium and vitamin supply.

In composition, the diet is ordinarily similar to that of the parents. Young carnivorous lizards are fed smaller prey than the adults.

> **TIP**
>
> ### Sex Determination
>
> For lizards with distinct dimorphism, that is, with visible distinctions between male and female, determining sex by external markings of mature animals is easy. With the beginning of sexual maturity, the males of some species grow flaps of skin or combs of varying sizes on their heads, throats, backs, or tails.
>
> Other visible differences are the preanal or femoral pores, which are more pronounced in male geckos, iguanas, and agamas than in the females.
>
> Much experience is needed to determine sex from the shape of the root of the tail. With many lizards, sex determination is only possible through the use of a probe; for this, you should definitely consult an experienced lizard-keeper.

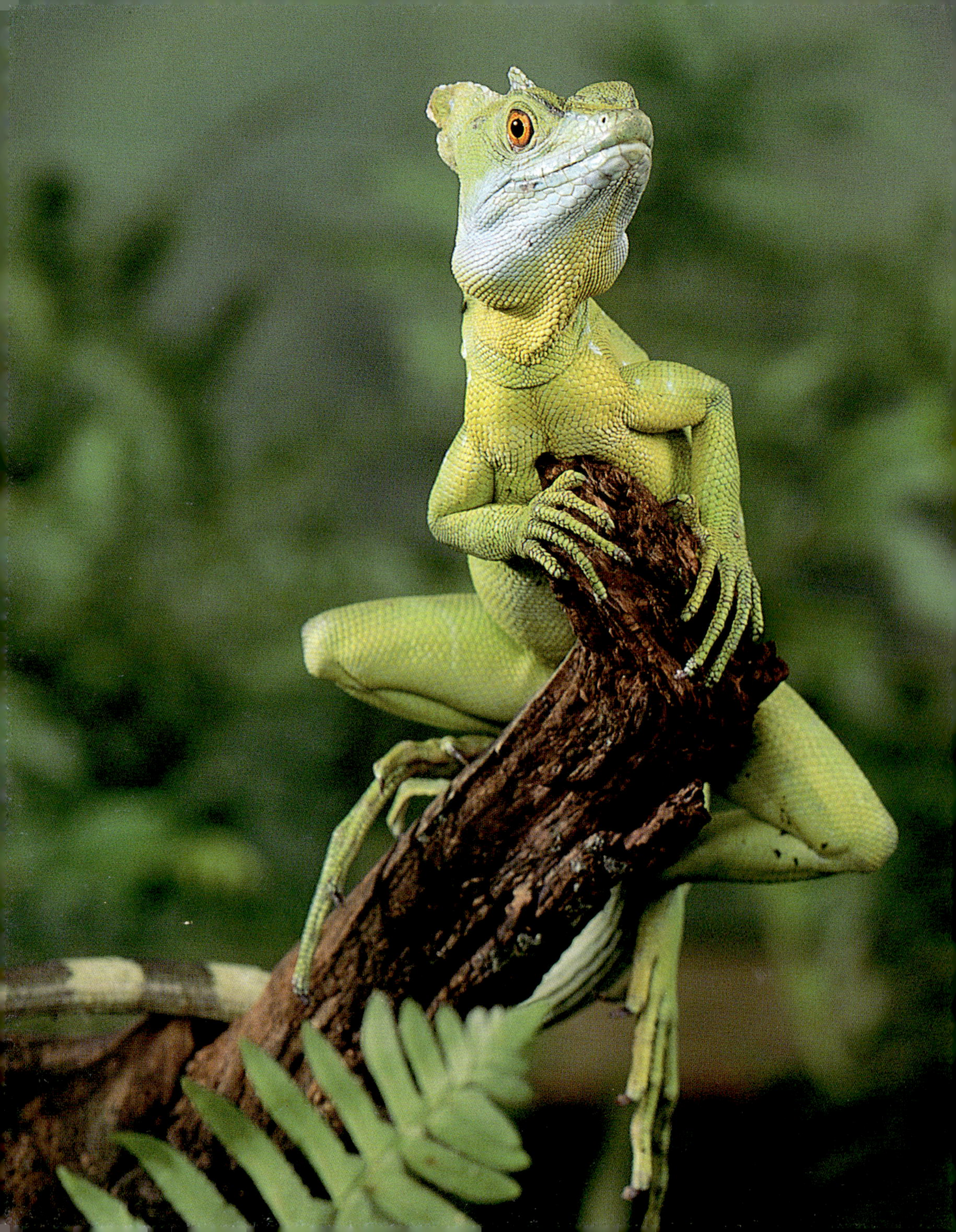

OBSERVING AND UNDERSTANDING LIZARDS

In the course of their evolution, as they adapted to a wide variety of habitats, lizards have developed interesting physical features and behavior patterns. As you enjoy observing these in the terrarium, you can even learn to interpret the mood of your lizard or tell if it is under stress.

Body Temperature

Lizards are described as cold-blooded animals, because their body temperature is influenced by the temperature of their surroundings. Unlike mammals and birds, they have little or no means of keeping their body temperature constant. For example, a dark-colored lizard absorbs much warmth from the sun as it basks. Its body temperature can be even higher than the ambient temperature. If the heat of the sun becomes too great, lizards seek shade or cool, damp hollows in the earth.

The Limbs

✔ Tree-dwelling, fast-climbing species have long, delicately jointed legs—especially the tibia (shinbone). These lizards have extremely long feet and long toes, which are armed with sharp claws.
✔ Some also have fringes of skin on the toes that enable the lizard to scamper on its two hind legs across the surface of the water (see photo, page 37).

Tree-dwelling lizards like the green basilisk have delicately jointed toes.

✔ Terrestrial lizards, like the skinks, are generally robust, with short, powerful limbs and sturdy feet. Many of them can dig holes and tunnels in the earth.
✔ Special adaptations are the adhesive lamellae (platelike growths) on the undersides of the toes of most geckos. Microscopic hooked cells on the lamellae enable geckos to maintain a grip on smooth surfaces such as large leaves, ceilings, and even on glass.

The Skin

In most lizards the skin is highly developed. It consists of scales and sometimes bony plates of different sizes, shapes, and arrangement. Occasionally, the lizard molts—it sheds the old skin, replacing it with a new and somewhat larger skin. The fast-growing young lizard molts at shorter intervals than older lizards.

Although *molting* is governed by the hormones of the pituitary and thyroid glands, external factors like temperature, humidity, food supply, and the lizard's overall condition also play a role. Molting proceeds differently among various species of lizards:
✔ Skinks slip out of their skin like a snake and leave it behind all in one piece.

Observing and Understanding Lizards

> ## TIP
>
> **Observing Lizards**
>
> Lizards, even if they have been bred for several generations in the terrarium, carry the long heritage of their wild forebears.
>
> Keeping lizards is a responsible undertaking, demanding specific knowledge of their life needs. This knowledge can be gained from books and magazines and from association with other lizard-keepers—but the lizards themselves are also excellent teachers. You need only to learn to understand them.
>
> Begin by taking the time to observe your lizards. Write down whatever you see that seems important. In time, you will learn to interpret your observations, to recognize certain behavior patterns, and to distinguish behavior that is normal from behavior that is unusual. This will help you give your lizards proper care.

✔ Other lizards, like the monitors, lose their skin in patches or shreds.
✔ Geckos grasp the old skin in their mouth, pull it from the body, and eat it, thereby taking in valuable nutrients.

The *changing color of the skin* is brought about by the expansion and contraction of the pigment in the color cells of the dermis and lower epidermis. The color change is controlled by hormones or by the nervous system. It is a reaction to the mood and temperature of the lizard. Threats, displaying, courtship, or mating can influence the color range of many lizard species.

The Sense Organs

Eyes: In most lizards, the sense of sight is very well developed, even allowing them to perceive colors. Evidence for this comes principally from the body language through which lizards identify each other or communicate. In species active at night, the pupils contract to a slit-shape during the day. As light dims, the slit widens.

Ears: Hearing abilities vary from species to species. Geckos have comparatively good hearing; the sounds and cries that they emit during mating, particularly, are an indication of this.

Tongue: Aromatic substances are taken onto the tongue tip when the tongue is extended and are deposited into the roof of the mouth where the Jacobson's organ is located. The perception of the aromatic substance is accomplished through the sensory-cell tissue of this organ. Therefore, increased darting of the tongue—at feeding, for example—is analogous to the excited sniffing of a dog.

After eating, many lizards polish their mouth with their tongue. Almost all use it to lap up water. Geckos regularly clean their eyes with their fleshy tongues (see photo, page 48). The monitor lizard has a notch in the upper jaw that allows its tongue to dart even when the jaws are closed (see drawing, page 47).

Typical Features and Behavior Patterns

Lizard species vary not only in their physical features, but also in their behavior. Some particularly striking behavior patterns are easy to observe in the terrarium.

Note: It is particularly important for the lizard-keeper to recognize threatening behavior, because the threat may also be directed against the keeper. In that case, special caution

//
Observing Lizard Behavior

is required. An iguana or a larger monitor can bite or deliver a painful tail swipe—even the smaller Tokay gecko has a fierce bite.

Family: Gecko (Gekkonidae)

Almost all the members of this family have adhesive lamellae on the undersides of their toes; exceptions include the fat-tailed, leopard, and Western banded geckos. Geckos pay special attention to cleaning their toes during molting (see pages 35, 59).

Threatening behavior: Tokays threaten with a wide-open mouth that reveals the colors of the throat. The vibrating tip of a leopard gecko's tail betrays agitation or tension.

Social behavior: Almost all geckos live in loose groups. Every animal has its own defined territory but also needs the nearness of other geckos, which it greets on the border, threatens, or courts.

Family: Agama (Agamidae)

Dewlaps and crests are primarily seen in males. If they are present in both sexes, they are noticeably larger in the male.

Threatening behavior: Agamas threaten by nodding their heads or presenting the trunk vertical and flattened; bearded lizards threaten with wide-open mouth and their prickly black beard—a fold of skin on the neck—erected.

Social behavior: You can keep sailfin lizards and water dragons in family groups. However, males of the same species must be housed separately or else the lower-ranking lizard will be overly stressed and will die.

Note for care: Sailfin lizards and water dragons are nervous animals that are quick to flee. They do not recognize glass and jump against it or constantly rub their snouts against it, damaging their lips and jaws. Partially paint or otherwise coat the glass so it is visible.

Monitor lizards threaten their rivals by high-stepping with trunk and neck puffed large.

BEHAVIOR GUIDE

To give your lizard proper care, you must be able to interpret important behavior patterns.

👉 *This is what my lizard is doing.*

❓ *What does it mean?*

❗ *Here's what to do!*

👉 Day gecko licks its lips and eyes.
❓ This is normal after eating.
❗ Check anyway—are the eyes healthy?

👉 Anole erects the dewlap on its throat.
❓ Male courtship or threatening behavior.
❗ Watch to see whether lizards mate.

👉 Chameleon with very dark background color.
❓ Pregnant female. Keep separated!
❗ Lay down firm substrate, 4 inches (10 cm) thick. Female will dig holes to lay her eggs.

👉 Chameleon with short crest and heel spurs.
❓ Young male lizard.
❗ Do not keep in company with older male.

👆 Adhesive lamellae enable climbing geckos to grip smooth surfaces.
❓ Provide terrarium plants with large leaves.
❗ If the lizard can't grip, it may need help with molting.

👆 Water dragon on a sunny branch.
❓ It's enjoying a sunbath.
❗ Use heat lamps to provide basking spots for other lizards as well.

Tokay threatens by displaying throat color. Watch out—it may bite! 👆
Stop working in the terrarium. ❗

👆 Young common iguana clambers among thin branches.
❓ The toes can't grip well.
❗ Install stout, sturdier limbs.

👆 House gecko, camouflaged on tree bark.
❓ The background provides safety.
❗ Create such places for lizards to hide.

Observing and Understanding Lizards

> ## TIP
>
> ### Housing Lizards Together
>
> If you wish to keep several lizards in the same terrarium, you should observe the following guidelines:
>
> ✔ To keep larger numbers of lizards, it's simplest to choose lizards of a single species that live gregariously or in loose groups (see Species Profiles, pages 10–20).
>
> ✔ Housing lizards of different species together can cause stress situations in the terrarium (see page 51). Therefore, it's essential to keep close watch; a dominated lizard that hides out of sight will soon languish. The table on page 19 lists species that may get along in shared quarters.
>
> ✔ The best plan is to install a group of lizards in the fresh territory of a new terrarium setup. By all means, avoid introducing one new lizard into an already established group.

Family: Iguana (Iguanidae)

Most iguanas have dewlaps and crests on the head, back, or tail. Such features are often more pronounced in the males. Members of this small family range in size from 18 to 72 inches (47–190 cm) and are adapted to deserts, islands, or jungle/savanna.

Threatening behavior: To identify and defend their territory, and when mating, iguanas walk stiff-legged with mouth wide open and trunk flattened from side to side to look larger. Adult pet male green iguanas can be very aggressive toward humans.

Social behavior: Most male common iguanas cannot be kept together in a single terrarium. Besides the physical stress, the psychological stress is too great for the lower-ranked lizard. It is possible for different species to share a terrarium.

Family: Corytophanidae

Basilisks are active tree-climbers who are usually found at low heights, over water. When frightened, they run on their hind legs, even over water. They have cranial crests and neck pouches.

Note for care: Basilisks act extremely frightened during their initial adjustment period in a terrarium. They jump against the glass, which is invisible to them, and injure their snouts. Therefore, you should cover most of the glass with paper or drape fabric around it.

Family: Polychrotidae

Anoles are small to good-sized lizards [6–18 inches (16–47 cm)]. Some can change color from green to brown and back again. All anoles have an erectile dewlap, but that of the female is smaller and less brightly colored.

Family: Skink (Scincidae)

Skinks have a cylindrical body with mostly smooth, shiny scales. Because their limbs are very short, skinks progress with a creeping motion.

The chameleon's darting tongue, almost as long as its body, captures insect prey.

Observing Lizard Behavior

Threatening behavior: Skinks threaten by opening the mouth wide. Blue-tongued skinks exhibit their shimmering gray-blue tongue and the red mucous membrane of their mouth.

Social behavior: Skinks, though placid in isolation, need ample space in shared quarters, because they are very aggressive toward each other. If you need to separate them to keep the peace, remove the dominant, stronger lizard (see *Housing Lizards Together,* page 50).

Family: Monitors (Varanidae)

Many characteristics of monitors remind one of snakes. The motion is slithering, and the deeply cleft tongue is continually stretched out to take up scent particles. When the throat is expanded, large pieces of food can be swallowed whole.

Threatening behavior: Monitor lizards signal an attack by high-stepping with head sunk and agitated puffing-up of trunk and neck (see drawing, page 47).

Social behavior: Most monitors are solitary; it may be possible to keep a family group in a shared terrarium, but never put two males together.

Warning: Be particularly careful in dealing with monitors; they can inflict deep bite wounds. Newly introduced animals are especially frightened and move very fast. A monitor will defend itself fiercely not only with its teeth, but also with its tail and claws. If you are injured, seek immediate medical attention (see *Important Notes,* page 63).

Avoiding Stressful Situations in the Terrarium

Only a lizard-keeper who is familiar with the lizards' everyday behavior will be able to recognize when a lizard is undergoing a stress situation. If a lizard is constantly threatened by one of the others, or seems to be languishing under pressure, the keeper must intervene at once.

✔ By increasing the size and number of rocks, plants and branches, you can provide barriers that provide the dominated lizard with its own territory. If this is not possible, the lizards must be separated.

✔ You should avoid introducing a new lizard into a terrarium in which the inhabitants have already established their own territories. If this cannot be avoided, it may help if you remove the original lizards from the terrarium until the new occupant has had a chance to settle in. Usually, however, the old inhabitants continue to dominate, for they recognize their familiar scent signals. In that case, your only option is to clean and rearrange the terrarium completely.

✔ If you house several lizards in the same terrarium, be sure that the space is ample for their needs (see TIP: *Terrarium Size,* page 11).

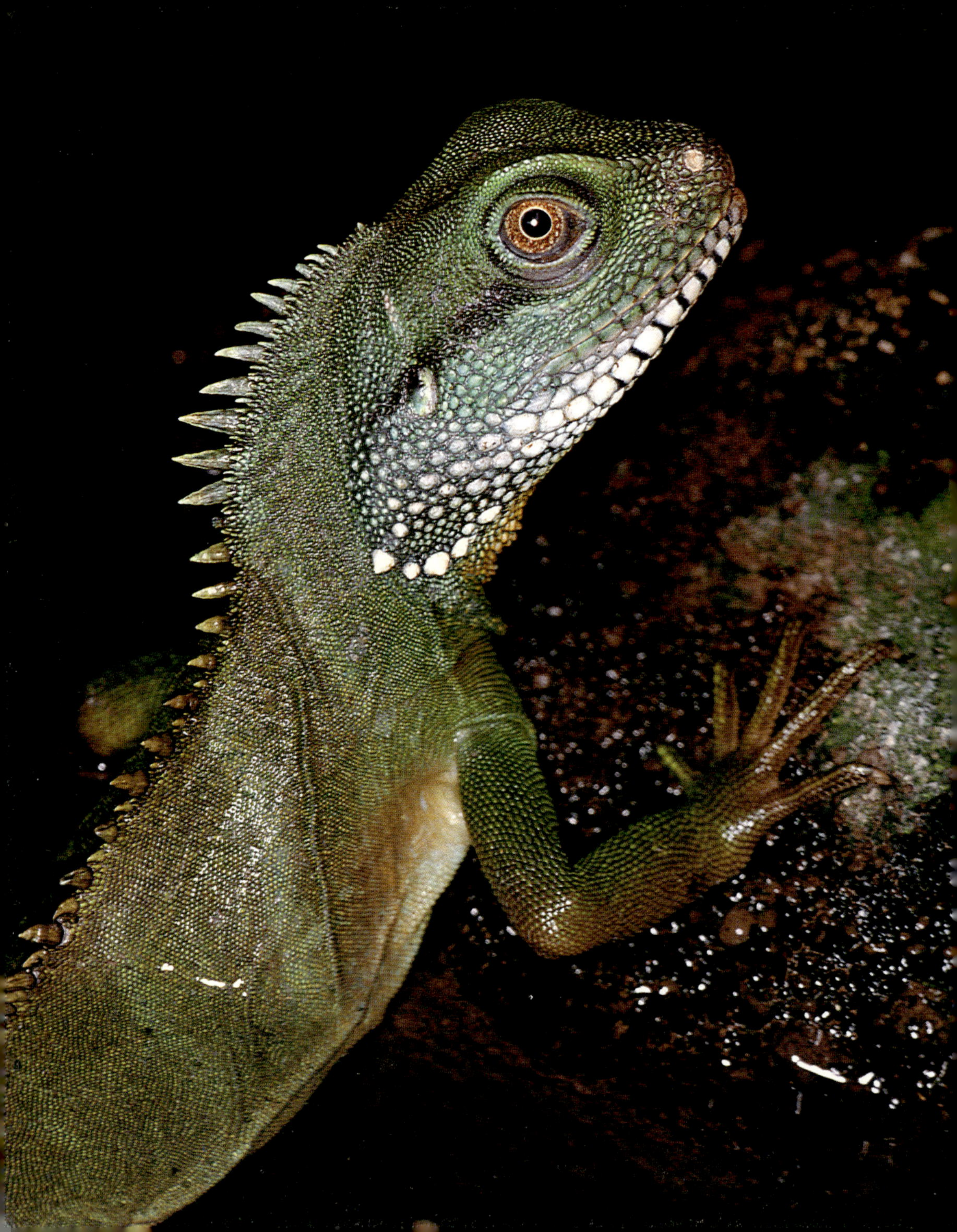

PREVENTIVE CARE AND HEALTH PROBLEMS

Lizards are exposed to many stressful situations and possible infections. To prevent illness, you must give your lizards proper care and attention. A clean terrarium and living conditions that closely resemble their natural habitat are the first prerequisites for healthy lizards.

Your Lizard's Health

Though you can never completely simulate the conditions of "living free in the wild," it's essential to provide both proper nourishment and the right climate, landscape features, and living space in the terrarium. Be sure you are very familiar with what your lizards need, and always observe your lizards carefully. An ailment is usually evident in changed appearance and/or behavior.

As soon as you suspect illness, take the affected lizard to the veterinarian. Never experiment yourself! Although the treatment of reptiles is not generally part of veterinary practice, the veterinarian has experience in handling animals in general. He or she can show you how the treatment procedures should be performed, and supply or prescribe the necessary medications. Don't take it upon yourself to administer continued low doses of medications as "prevention." Surgical procedures and injections, obviously, should only be undertaken by the veterinarian. You and the veterinarian may also want to consult an experienced hobbyist or breeder (see page 62).

Have the veterinarian do a fecal examination at four-week intervals during the quarantine period, and once a year for acclimated lizards (see TIP: *Fecal Examinations,* page 55).

Note: A lizard that is showing signs of possible illness must be removed from the terrarium and placed in quarantine quarters to protect the health of the other animals (see page 23).

Handling Lizards Correctly

To treat a sick lizard, but also for claw-trimming or force-feeding, it is necessary to take the lizard in your hand and hold it so that neither human nor lizard can come to harm.

Small to medium-size lizards must be grasped quickly and with sure aim. Thumb and forefinger of one hand hold the lizard firmly behind the head so that it can't bite. The palm lies on the lizard's back; the three free fingers grasp the legs from underneath and fix them toward the back-swept hips and tail (see drawing, page 54). Thus, the lizard cannot bite and

Water dragons are native to tropical rainforests and like to swim.

scratch, and it is not in danger of losing its tail or injuring it by wild thrashing. The necessary measures can then be administered with the other hand.

Larger lizards are virtually impossible to hold with one hand; to treat them, you will need a helper. With one hand, the keeper holds the neck, the head, and the front legs; the other hand grasps the tail area and holds the rear legs at the same time (see drawing, page 55).

To hold a small lizard, grasp the head between thumb and forefinger as shown.

For a large and aggressive lizard, the tail must also be immobilized by being grasped firmly between the keeper's legs. All the necessary ministrations to the lizard are carried out by the second person.

Note: When working about a lizard's head, it can be very helpful to enclose the lizard's trunk and tail in a sturdy cotton or muslin sack. Use extreme caution nevertheless, because long claws can still penetrate the sack and can cause injuries.

Treating Illnesses

For a summary of the causes and symptoms of common ailments, see the table on page 58.

External Parasites

Mites are pinhead-sized black parasites. They live on the blood of their host, biting the softer parts of the skin under the scales. The infestation causes general weakness and stress from the constant itching.

Treatment: Remove the water container from cage. Hang a 1 inch (2.6 cm) square piece of insect strip (available at pet shops) in the terrarium; leave in place for three days. Remove the insect strip; replace the water. Repeat after seven days.

Ticks are tiny flat arthropods, up to ¼ inch (6 mm) in size. They attach themselves firmly under the scales on the soft skin parts and suck the lizard's blood.

Treatment: Same as for mites.

Pneumonia

Lung infections, usually caused by bacteria, are promoted by terrarium conditions that are too warm or too cool. Lowered resistance because of age or stress can also be a factor. Activity and food intake are considerably reduced.

Treatment: Only by a veterinarian, who will prescribe the needed medication.

Also review terrarium conditions and care:
✔ Make sure the terrarium is both properly heated during the day and cooler at night (see Species Profiles, pages 10–20). Constant temperature conditions lead to sickly lizards.

Treating Illnesses

TIP

Fecal Examinations

Certain internal illnesses and parasites can be recognized early through fecal examinations, facilitating prompt treatment of any ailments. During the quarantine period for new lizards, have examinations three times at intervals of four weeks. For acclimated lizards, stool samples should be tested once a year. It's important to collect stool samples while they are fresh, preferably still moist, and to submit them immediately for analysis by a veterinarian.

✔ Monitor your lizards' food intake and digestion, because lizards can be weakened by intestinal parasites.
✔ Review the dosage of mineral and vitamin supplements; give additional vitamins during and after treatment.

Mouth Rot

Following respiratory and gastrointestinal illnesses, deposits may form in the lizard's mouth, irritating the mucous membranes. Bite wounds, improper care, and malnutrition also promote these mouth infections.

Treatment: Multivitamin drops and daily cleaning with cotton swabs dipped in chamomile tea may suffice to eliminate the cheesy mucus or secretion. If not, the veterinarian must test the secretion and prescribe an appropriate antibiotic. Review terrarium hygiene and care.

Swollen Eyes

Vitamin deficiencies can lead to swelling, which usually affects both eyes.

If the eye or eyelid is reddened, suspect inflammation, possibly caused by the intensity of UV lights, especially if actin or halogen bulbs are used.

Treatment: The veterinarian will administer eyedrops and inject a vitamin preparation.
✔ Then you should give a multivitamin preparation daily for at least four weeks.
✔ Review terrarium hygiene and care.
✔ Possibly reduce UV lighting.

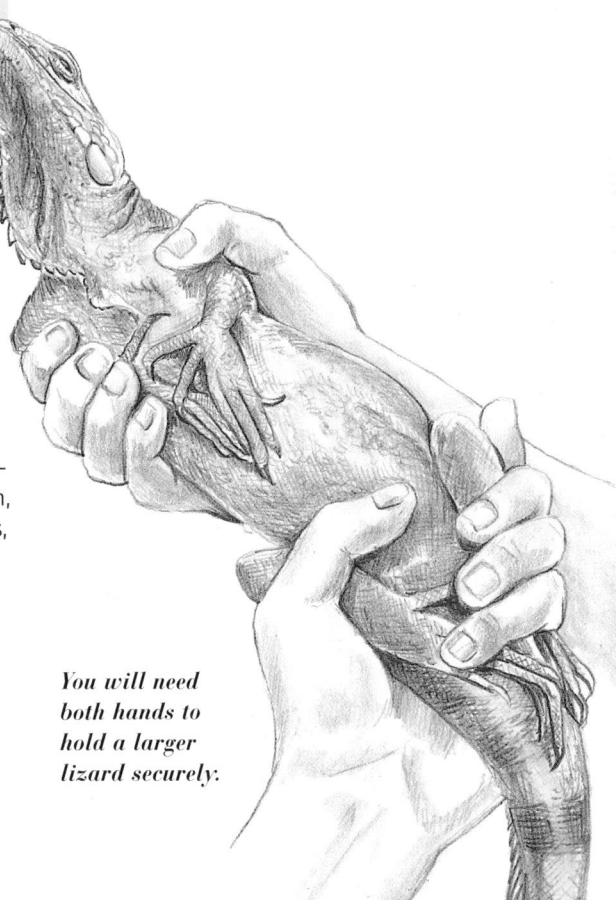

You will need both hands to hold a larger lizard securely.

Preventive Care and Health Problems

Bite Wounds

Large wounds need veterinary attention. You can treat smaller wounds yourself.

Treatment:

✔ Clean and disinfect the wound.
✔ Apply antibiotic cream or powder. Do not use adhesive tape or bandages; a liquid skin bandage will help prevent the entrance of dirt or bacteria.
✔ Keep wounded lizards under sterile conditions in a quarantine terrarium.
✔ Remove aggressive lizards from the terrarium and reconsider the group structure. You may have too many lizards in too little space. It's also common for competing males to injure one another.

Skin Necrosis

Abscesses may form as a result of injuries or metabolic disorders.

Treatment: The veterinarian lances the abscess and treats the wound. Make sure vitamin levels and UV lighting are sufficient, and review terrarium hygiene.

Skin Fungi

Skin fungi are promoted by unfavorable climatic conditions, mostly too cool and too damp.

Treatment: Large, flat patches of darkened, or otherwise unhealthy-looking skin, without the development of pus, call for prompt veterinary care. Often an effective medication will not be found on the first attempt. Treatment usually takes a long time and requires quarantine under sterile conditions. Review climatic conditions in the terrarium.

Metabolic Bone Disease

Insufficient calcium is the cause of metabolic bone disease, a type of rickets. Too little calcium and/or vitamin D in the diet, too little UV irradiation, but also improper nutrition and excessively high temperatures in the terrarium can produce the rachitic deficiencies, a progressive and often fatal disease.

Treatment: Check for the possible causes listed above. Improve calcium and vitamin supply.

Convulsive Trembling

In the early stages, only insignificant vibration is noticeable. Later the whole body obviously trembles, especially if the lizard is alarmed by contact. The lizard can no longer flee and climb.

Treatment: The veterinarian will first inject high doses of vitamin B_1. This is followed by daily oral doses of vitamin B_1.

The golddust day gecko lives on palm trees and feeds on insects.

Treating Illnesses

The leopard gecko lives in dry regions. It shelters in cool caves during the day, becoming active as dusk falls.

Circulatory Disorders of Tail and Toes

A diet that is too rich in protein and low in fiber and minerals can lead to a circulatory disorder, much like gout, that causes the tail and toes to dry out.

Treatment: Dead tissue in the toes or tail must be removed by the veterinarian, who will amputate to where the blood supply is adequate. Correct the lizard's diet.

Intestinal or Penis Prolapse

Only rarely seen in lizards. A portion of the intestine or hemipenis is extruded at the cloacal vent. Immediate attention is needed or the extruded portion will dry out.

Treatment: The veterinarian will try to massage the extrusion back into place. If this is not successful, amputation is the only option.

Vomiting

A single instance of vomiting is not cause for concern. Repeated vomiting may indicate poisoning, but this is difficult to prove.

Treatment: Review care, particularly food quantity, and watch for disturbances and stress factors.

Intestinal Disorders

Many ailments cannot be detected in their early stages with the naked eye. This is especially true of intestinal disorders. Only rarely,

Preventive Care and Health Problems

Recognizing Health Problems

Symptoms	Causes
Bubbles at the nostrils, jerky opening and closing of the mouth, rattling breath sounds	Lung infection (pneumonia)
Deposits of dried mucus, abscesses, patches of dead tissue in mouth	Mouth rot
Weepy, swollen eyes	Inflammation caused by drafts, burning caused by excessive/high intensity UV irradiation
Skin and flesh wounds	Bite injuries
Skin necrosis (abscesses)	Injuries, metabolic disorders
Scabby patches of skin	Skin fungi, promoted by excessive humidity
Gray-white deposits on the skin	Feces of mites
Small, flat, round objects attached to skin	Ticks
Curvature of the skeleton	Rachitic deficiencies, metabolic disorders, improper care
Trembling of limbs, tail, and trunk	Convulsive trembling caused by vitamin B_1 deficiency
Missing or dead toes	Crush injuries, molting residues
Drying out of tip of tail and/or toes	Circulatory disorder caused by improper diet
Tail broken off or damaged	Caught in terrarium decoration or by yanking by human
Body part protruding at cloacal vent	Intestinal or penis prolapse
Vomiting	Improper care, too much food or food particles too large, poisoning
Runny, bloody, foul-smelling feces; cloaca reddened, slimy	Inflammation of intestinal tract caused by bacterial or viral infection, parasites
Worms in feces	Intestinal parasites

in cases of severe infestation, will worms be visible in the fresh stool of lizards.

Treatment: Most of the infections and intestinal parasites that cause nutritional deprivation, toxic effects, and inflammation of the intestinal wall can be identified only by fecal examinations (see TIP, page 55). The results should diagnose the parasite, as being amoebae, flagellates, tapeworms, roundworms, pinworms, or nematodes.

Any amoebic infestation must be promptly and thoroughly eliminated because it can wipe out all your lizards. After conclusion of the treatment, the lizards should be monitored with fecal examinations (at least six, at regular intervals).

Molting Problems

Molting difficulties may be caused by improper conditions such as humidity that is too low or too high, by disturbance of general health, by an attack of external parasites, or by vitamin deficiencies. You may see some skin remaining at the ends of the toes or at the tail tip of a lizard afflicted with molting problems (see *Grooming*, page 35). Abnormally frequent shedding may result from an overdosage of vitamin preparations.

Treatment:

✔ Review care and terrarium conditions, especially climate.

✔ Increase or decrease vitamin dosage, as needed.

✔ If skin residue remains on toes or tail, soak the extremity briefly in warm water, or allow lizard to run on damp bath toweling; then remove any remnants of skin.

✔ Keeping a log of your observations will help you to distinguish normal from abnormal molting behavior.

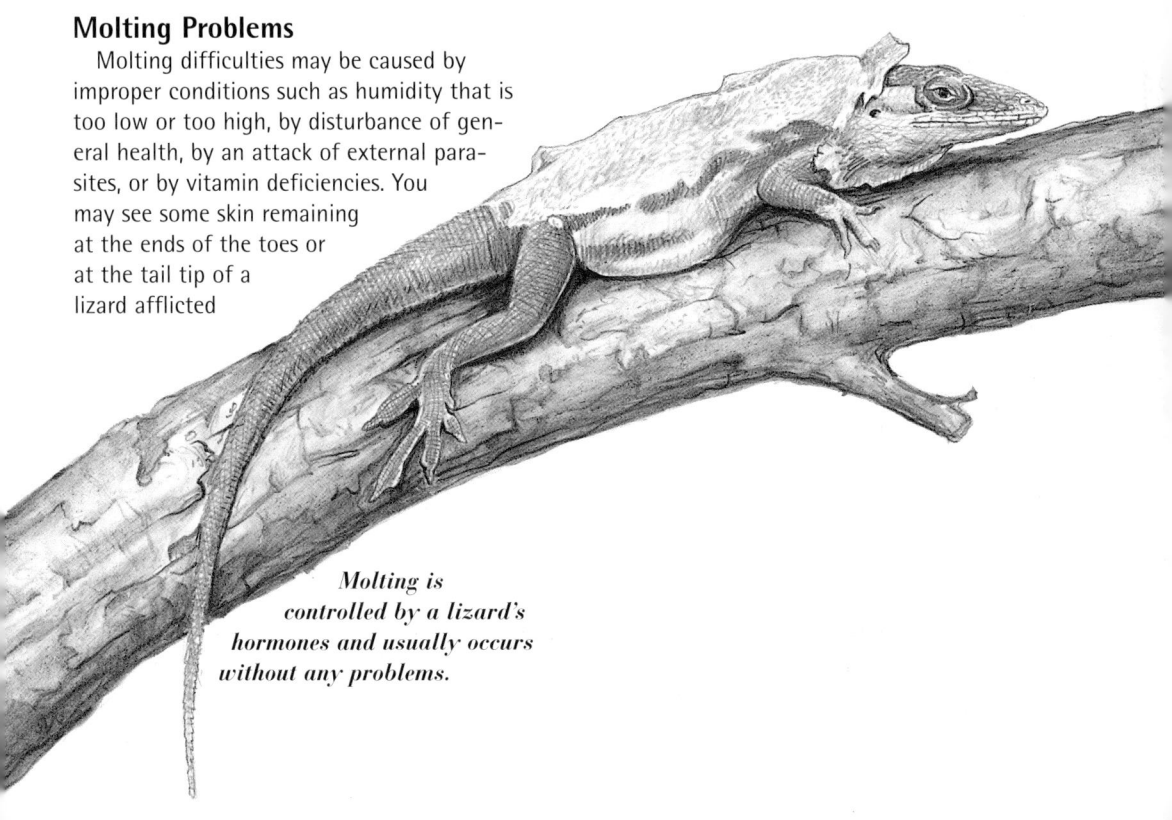

Molting is controlled by a lizard's hormones and usually occurs without any problems.

INDEX

Abscess, 56, 58
Agama family:
  behavior patterns of, 47
  characteristic features of, 47
  courtship patterns, 40
  Spiny-tailed Agamid, 18–19, 61
Anatomy:
  limbs, 45
  sense organs, 46
  skin, 45–46
Anoles:
  characteristic features of, 50
  courtship patterns, 40
  Knight, 11
Aphids, 36, 39

Banded Gecko, 12, 19
Basilisks:
  behavior patterns of, 50
  characteristic features of, 50
  Common, 17, 19
  Green, 17, 19, 37
Behavior
  guidelines for observing, 48–49
  nocturnal, 64
  patterns of, 46–47
Bite wounds, 51, 56, 65
Body temperature, 45
Branches, 31
Breeding:
  courtship, 40
  mating, 40
  overview of, 40
Buying:
  checklist for, 21
  considerations before, 6–7, 46
  health evaluation before, 21

prices, 65
sources for, 21
transportation after, 22

Carnivores, 22, 38–39
Characteristics, 4
Circulatory disorders, 57
Claws, 35
Cleaning, 34
Climbing, 23, 31
Cloaca, 40
Cockroaches, 36, 39
Collared Lizard, 12, 14
Common Basilisk, 17, 19
Common House Gecko, 9–10, 12, 19
Conservation efforts, 15
Convulsive trembling, 56
Corytophanidae family, 50
Courtship, 40
Crevice Spiny Lizard, 14
Crickets, 36, 39

Desert terrarium:
  how to make, 30
  water in, 39
Diet. see also Feeding
  insects, 36
  minerals, 37
  plants in, 36
  vitamins, 37
  for young lizards, 43

Ears, 46
Eastern Water Dragon, 17, 20
Eggs:
  incubator placement, 40–42
  laying of, 40
Emerald Monitor, 20
Eyes:
  anatomy of, 46
  swollen, 55, 58

Fat-tail Gecko, 11–12, 19
Feces:
  examination of, 55
  worms in, 58
Feeding. see also Diet
  after birth, 43
  carnivorous lizards, 22, 38–39
  considerations for, 22–23
  force-feeding, 38
  herbivorous lizards, 38
  timing of, 38
Fish, 36
Floor covering, 23
Floor heating, 23
Fluorescent lamps, 26
Force-feeding, 38
Fruits, 36

Gecko family:
  Banded Gecko, 12, 19
  behavior patterns of, 47
  characteristic features of, 47
  Common House Gecko, 9–10, 12, 19
  Fat-tail Gecko, 11–12, 19
  Golddust Day Gecko, 10, 19, 56
  Leopard Gecko, 12, 19, 57
  Lined Gecko, 18
  Madagascar Day Gecko, 10–11, 13
  molting, 46
  Striped Day Gecko, 10, 19
  Tokay Gecko, 18, 24
Golddust Day Gecko, 10, 19, 56
Green Basilisk, 17, 19, 37

Green Iguana, 15, 19
Green Spiny Lizard, 13–14
Grooming, 35

Haitian Curlytail Lizard, 14, 19, 42
Halogen lamps, 26
Handling, 53–54
Health. see also Illnesses
  evaluation before buying, 21
  guidelines for maintaining, 33
  maintenance of, 53
Heating, 23, 26
Hemipenes, 40, 57
Herbivores, 38
Hiding places, 23, 30
History, 9
Housing. see Terrarium
Humidity, 27, 34

Iguana family:
  behavior patterns of, 50
  characteristic features of, 50
  courtship patterns, 40
  Green Iguana, 15, 19
Illnesses. see also Health
  circulatory disorders of tail and toes, 57
  convulsive trembling, 56
  handling considerations, 53–54
  intestinal disorders, 57, 59
  metabolic bone disease, 56
  parasites, 54
  penis prolapse, 57
  pneumonia, 54–55

Index

skin fungi, 56
skin necrosis, 56
symptoms of, 58
vomiting, 57–58
Information sources, 62
Infrared lamps, 26
Inland Bearded Dragon, 13, 21
Insects:
 feeding of, 38–39
 types of, 36
Intestinal disorders, 57, 59
Intestinal prolapse, 57

Knight anole, 11

Lamps:
 for heating, 26
 for lighting, 26–27
Leopard Gecko, 12, 19, 57
Life expectancy, 64
Lighting:
 for plants, 28
 for terrarium, 23, 26–27
Lined Gecko, 18
Live-bearing lizards, 42–43

Madagascar Day Gecko, 10–11, 13
Mating, 40
Metabolic bone disease, 56
Minerals, 37
Mites, 22, 54
Molting, 35, 45, 59
Monitor family:
 behavior patterns of, 51
 characteristic features of, 51
 Emerald Monitor, 20

Ridgetail Monitor, 16, 21
Spotted Tree Monitor, 17, 20
Mountain Horned Dragon, 17–18
Mouth rot, 55

Parasites, 54
Pink-tongued Skink, 20
Plants:
 care for, 27
 desert, 27–30
 in diet, 36
 rainforest, 32
 selection of, 27
Pneumonia, 54–55
Polychrotidae family, 50

Quarantine terrarium, 22–23
Questions commonly asked, 64–65

Rainforest terrarium:
 how to make, 30–31
 water in, 39
Reflector lamps, 26
Rice, 36
Ridgetail Monitor, 16, 21
Rocks, 26

Sailfin Lizard, 15, 19
Sense organs, 46
Sex determination, 43
Shedding of skin. *see* Molting
Skin:
 anatomy of, 45–46
 color changes of, 46
 conditions that affect, 56, 58
 fungi, 56
 molting of, 35, 45, 59, 64
 necrosis of, 56
Skink family:
 behavior patterns of, 51
 characteristic features of, 50–51
 molting, 45
 Pink-tongued Skink, 20
 Solomon Island Skink, 19–20
Slugs, 38
Snails, 36, 38
Solomon Island Skink, 19–20
Spiders, 36
Spiny-tailed Agamid, 18–19, 61
Spotted Tree Monitor, 17, 20

Striped Day Gecko, 10, 19
Sun terrarium, 31
Supplements, 37, 39
Swollen eyes, 55, 58

Tail, circulatory disorders of, 57–58
Temperature:
 body, 45
 for incubating eggs, 41
 terrarium, 27, 34
 for transportation, 22
 vacation considerations, 35
Terrarium:
 cleaning of, 34
 desert, 30
 electrical precautions, 63
 floor covering for, 23
 heating of, 23, 26
 hiding places in, 23, 30
 humidity of, 27, 34
 legal considerations, 65
 lighting of, 23, 26–27
 location for, 25
 maintenance of, 34–35
 multiple lizards in, 50
 plants in, 27–32
 quarantine, 22–23
 rainforest, 30–31
 shape of, 25
 size of, 9, 11, 25

The spiny-tailed agamid enjoys a good sunbath.

INFORMATION

species-based
   considerations, 19
stress reductions in, 51
sun, 31
temperature of, 27, 34
ventilation for, 25
water container, 23, 31
young lizards in, 42
Territoriality, 51
Thermostats, 27
Ticks, 22, 54
Toes, circulatory
   disorders of, 57–58
Tokay Gecko, 18, 24
Tongue, 46
Transportation, 22
Trembling, 56
Trimming of claws, 35

Ultraviolet lighting,
   26–27

Vacation, 35
Vegetables, 36
Veiled Chameleon,
   12–13, 17
Ventilation, 25
Vitamins, 37
Vomiting, 57–58

Water:
   changing of, 35
   containers for, 23, 31
   misting, 39
Water Dragon, 13,
   16–17
Worms, 36

Young lizard, 42

Useful Addresses

- Society for the Study of Amphibians
and Reptiles (SSAR)
Department of Zoology
Miami University
Oxford, OH 45056

- Herpetologist's League
C/O Texas National
   Heritage Program
Texas Parks and Wildlife Department
4200 Smith School Road
Austin, TX 78744

Useful Books

(Look for these at your bookstore or library.)
Bartlett, Richard and Patti Bartlett. *Anoles, Basilisks, and Water Dragons: A Complete Pet Owner's Manual.* Hauppauge, NY: Barron's Educational Series, Inc., 1997.
_____. *Chameleons: A Complete Pet Owner's Manual.* Hauppauge, NY: Barron's Educational Series, Inc., 1997.
_____. *Lizard Care From A-To-Z.* Hauppauge, NY: Barron's Educational Series, Inc., 1997.
_____. *Monitors, Tegus and Related Lizards: A Complete Pet Owner's Manual.* Hauppauge, NY: Barron's Educational Series, Inc., 1996.
_____. *Iguanas: A Complete Pet Owner's Manual.* Hauppauge, NY: Barron's Educational Series, Inc., 1995.
Jes, Harald. *The Terrarium: A Complete Pet Owner's Manual.* Hauppauge, NY: Barron's Educational Series, Inc., 1998.
Manning, David. *Exotic Pets Handbook.* Hauppauge, NY: Barron's Educational Series, Inc., 1998.

Useful Magazines

Reptiles
P.O. Box 6050
Mission Viejo, CA 92690

Reptile and Amphibian Hobbyist
Third and Union Avenues
Neptune City, NJ 07753

About the Author

Harald Jes served for 26 years as director of the Aquarium am Zoo in Cologne, Germany, and was instrumental in its expansion and development. He has been involved with the care of reptiles for 40 years; his special interest lies in lizard breeding. He has also worked in his field as an educator and examiner of veterinary technicians.

Acknowledgment

The author and the publisher wish to thank attorney Reinhard Hahn for contributions on the topic of the law and the lizard owner.

About the Artist

Johann Brandstetter was trained as a restaurateur and artist. After accompanying biologists on research expeditions in Central Africa and Asia, he began to specialize in drawing plants and animals. For several years, he has illustrated books for notable publishers of nature books.

Photography Credits

Benyr: pages 12 bottom right, 16 bottom right, 17 bottom left, 53; Bilder Pur/Brakefield: page 48 bottom left; Bildur Pur/Galan: page 29 right; Bilder Pur/Lefevre/BIOS: pages 4–5; Bilder Pur/McDonald: pages 12 bottom left, 17 top left, top right, 25, 33 (small photo), 37, 44, 45; Bilder Pur/NAS/

Information

Detrick: page 8; blickwinkel/Klimmek: page 52; blickwinkel/Schröer: pages 13 bottom left, 40, 41 left, right, 48 top left, 49 top left, center right; blickwinkel/Ziegler: page 13 top right, 48 top right, 49 bottom left; Cramm: pages 49 top right, 57; Kahl: front cover (small photo), pages 9, 16 bottom left; Karbe: pages 16 top right, 48 bottom right; König: front cover (large photo), inside front cover, pages 12 top left, 33 (large photo), 61; Reinhard, Hans: pages 2–3, 12 top right, 13 top left, bottom right, 17 bottom right, 20, 24, 32, 49 bottom right, 56, 64–inside back cover, back cover; Reinhard, Nils: page 29 left; Schaefer: page 38; Trutnau: page 21; Ziehm: pages 6–7, 16 top left.

Photos on Book Cover, Title Page, Chapter Title Pages:

Front cover: Water dragon (large photo) and leopard gecko (small photo).
Back cover: Collared lizard.
Page 1: Common basilisk, prefers to climb on trees.
Pages 2–3: Day gecko.
Pages 4–5: Green basilisk.
Pages 6–7: Juvenile crevice spiny lizard.
Pages 64: Anole.

Important Note

All electrical equipment used in a terrarium must carry the UL symbol. Lamps that may be exposed to water or spray must be made with special safety glass. Disconnect the main electrical plug before you begin any work that involves water or touch any equipment. If the electrical current you use does not pass through a central fuse box or circuit breaker system, it is advisable to have a portable circuit breaker installed. Observe strict hygiene when handling lizards or their food animals. Always wash your hands well after contact with animals and plants; immediately rinse off any water that splashes onto your face. Teach your children to do the same. In case of injury, seek medical attention (see page 51).

English translation © Copyright 2000 by Barron's Educational Series, Inc.

Original title of the book in German is *Echsen*.

© Copyright 1999 by Gräfe und Unzer Verlag GmbH, Munich

English translation by Celia Bohannon.

All rights reserved.

No part of this book may be reproduced in any form, by photostat, microfilm, xerography, or any other means, or incorporated into any information retrieval system, electronic or mechanical, without the written permission of the copyright owner.

All inquiries should be addressed to:
Barron's Educational Series, Inc.
250 Wireless Boulevard
Hauppauge, New York 11788
http://www.barronseduc.com

Library of Congress Catalog Card No. 99-89584

International Standard Book Number 0-7641-1449-2

Library of Congress Cataloging-in-Publication Data
Jes, Harald.
 [Echsen. English]
  Lizards / Harald Jes ; illustrations by Johann Brandstetter.
  p. cm. – (A Complete pet owner's manual)
  Includes bibliographical references (p.).
  ISBN 0-7641-1449-2 (alk. paper)
  1. Lizards as pets. I. Title. II. Series.
SF459.L5 J4613 2000
639.3'95–dc21   99-89584

Printed in Hong Kong

9 8 7 6 5 4 3 2

ASK THE EXPERTS

1 Can lizards hear?

Certainly the species that emit sounds during courtship and when defending their territory can hear.

2 Why do lizards shed their skin?

Primarily to allow growth. Molting also regenerates the outer layer of skin.

3 If my lizard loses its tail, will it grow another?

Not with new bony tail vertebrae, but by developing new cartilage. The new tail is shorter, sometimes only a rounded knob.

4 How long do lizards live?

Crocodilians can live to be 50, 70, or even 100 years old. The lizards in this book may live up to 25 years.

5 Can nocturnal lizards be observed only at night?

Using a timer on the terrarium equipment makes it possible to adjust activity times so that you can observe these lizards in the evening (see page 27).

Experts answer the ten most common questions about lizard care.